D1090715

THE WORLD ART TOUR

Festivals

Architecture

Clothing and Fashion

Culinary Arts

Dance

Decorative Arts

Drawing and Painting

Festivals

Sculpture

THE WORLD ART TOUR
Festivals

BY Esther Lombardi

MASON CREST

Philadelphia • Miami

Mason Crest
450 Parkway Drive, Suite D
Broomall, PA 19008
(866) MCP-BOOK (toll free)
www.masoncrest.com

Printed in the United States of America

First printing
9 8 7 6 5 4 3 2 1

Series ISBN: 978-1-4222-4283-4
Hardcover ISBN: 978-1-4222-4290-2
ebook ISBN: 978-1-4222-7537-5

Cataloging-in-Publication Data is available on file
at the Library of Congress.

Developed and Produced by Print Matters Productions, Inc.
(www.printmattersinc.com)

Cover and Interior Design by Tom Carling, Carling Design, Inc.

CONTENTS

INTRODUCTION

Festivals are essential expressions of culture. They represent the identity of a country and a people. They remind us of where we came from and of our history and our values. These events tie us together as a community, allowing us to celebrate, grieve, and learn together. With masks, music, and extravagant displays, we step outside the realm of the everyday and into a time of myth and legend. Beyond the stories that bind us together, there's also a very personal, religious experience that's tied into festivals and celebrations.

WHAT'S MEMORY GOT TO DO WITH IT?

Festivals are not just about remembering the past and following the tenets of faith to bring about a feeling of hope and a promise for the future. They allow faith-based communities to collectively celebrate and remember the past in a real way, but these celebrations offer much more than just that. Beyond simple faith or belief, festivals can represent a substantiation of a lifelong dedication or purpose.

Masked characters are used to embody religious and historical figures from the past. Magic, myth, mystery, and heroism are all possible, real, and right out there in the open. We remember the miracles of saints and exploits of heroes, just as we honor the sacrifices of martyrs, both past and present. We also celebrate love and friendship. It's often trite to talk about love, but we tend to gravitate toward it for companionship, for human connection. We seek ways to explore the often-impossible-to-understand emotions, feelings, and relationships in our lives. And festivals give us something to look at, to explore, and to imagine.

Festivals mark the changing of the harvest and the seasons, helping us reflect upon ourselves and our place in the community. Through them, people immerse themselves in the ideals of Christmas, Diwali, Eid al-Adha, Rosh Hashanah, and so many other holidays. We need festivals. We need to belong. We need a space outside the norm that jolts us into a sense that what we have collectively accomplished as a people matters in the grander scheme of things.

WHAT DO WE LEARN?

Yes, festivals allow us to tap into the feeling that we belong to something bigger than ourselves. History, stories, language, culture—in many cases, we can't learn these culturally unique forms of social interaction or behavior anywhere else in the world. It's a social heritage that works on us beyond the confines of a single workshop or master class.

Festivals lay bare a body of knowledge that is essential from cultural and religious standpoints, but there's also a whole host of more seemingly innocuous ideas and concepts, tied up with attitudes, beliefs, customs, and morals. These are the unwritten learned and shared behaviors of a people, of shared experience, and of tolerance. If not for festivals, more of these most basic tenets would slip away.

WHY DO FESTIVALS MAKE US FEEL GOOD?

In the glow of celebratory intensity, endorphins flood our bodies. It's simple, and it's effective. Festivals, like most joyous events, typically help relieve stress and even counteract the effects of pain. One's blood pressure goes down. One's breathing evens out. We relax, our emotions balance out, and we smile.

That feel-good vibe is relaxing and washes away negativity, leaving a sense of overall well-being and happiness. That's just part of why festivals are embraced around the world. People want to feel good, but they also want to belong.

After all, at our very core we are social creatures, and a festival is the perfect opportunity to bring people together. For most events, it doesn't really matter what one's socioeconomic or religious background is. Everyone is on the same footing, on the same field, just swaying to the music or watching the dancers weave in and out in their ritualized movements. It's an intoxicating display. Our hope is that we will forget everyday concerns, if only for a few minutes or a day. It's a safe space, without fear or recrimination. It's about the here and now. It's about the beat.

WHY DO WE CARE?

Perhaps most important of all, festivals remind us that we care. In the humdrum chaos of life in modern society, it's easy to forget about what it means to be not only part of a community but also a part of history. We share stories, but we also collaborate in the social and cultural experiment that is our lives.

People care about each other—at least in some off-kilter, sideways way—and it is distressing when violence and hatred separate us. Festivals serve as a reminder that we can rise above the things that pull people apart. In these simple yet powerful events, we come together as friends, neighbors, and human beings. We meditate, pray, sing, and dance together. For a few minutes, days, or weeks, we forget that there is anything outside that feeling of belonging, hope, and joy. Although festivals may not save the world, they may provide the time and space to collectively remember what it feels like to come together for a common goal or purpose.

KEY TERMS

Aboriginal: A people who have lived or existed in a region for a long period of time, but also related to tribes, customs, and artistic endeavors.

Afrobeat: A music genre associated with West Africa, usually defined by a mix of American jazz, fuji, and funk influences; originated in Ghana around 1920s.

Alternative culture: The fringe of society, or outside of the mainstream; often associated with subcultures.

Belly dance: Undulating and rhythmic movement that originated in Egypt and is sometimes associated with the Middle East or Arabic culture.

Berber: The indigenous people located in North Africa (from Algeria, Morocco, or Tunisia); farmers or migrant workers.

Bonfire: A large controlled fire used for celebration, communal activities, or ritualistic purposes, derived from Celtic midsummer festivals and traditionally used to ward off evil spirits.

Decommodification: Sustained consumption, supporting a standard of living that is socially acceptable and sustainable; sometimes also refers to independent living, without requirements of money.

Folk festival: An event that usually focuses on the traditional music, crafts, and art of the local culture; artistic representation of the everyman.

Hallucinogenic: A substance that induces people to hear sounds, see lights, and feel sensations that aren't really there.

Harvest: The processing of gathering a crop; a supply of anything.

Indigenous: The people or things belonging or native to a place or region.

Krampus: A horned creature in Central European folklore and legend, often described as having the characteristics of a goat and demon.

Legend: A popular story that has been passed down; usually thought to be of historical significance but having no authenticity.

Lent: A time of fasting and penitence in the Christian religious tradition, beginning on Ash Wednesday and lasting up until Easter.

Nomadic: A tribe in the hunter-gathering tradition; a transient lifestyle that involves roaming, moving around, or even following the herds.

Oktoberfest: A festival in the fall or autumn, traditionally taking place in Germany, but with spin-off events taking place all over the world; often involves a celebration of the Bavarian culture, food, and drink.

Origin stories: The backstory or explanation of where the people come from, often with mythic or supernatural explanations for creation or evolution.

Pilgrimage: A religious expedition or journey to a sacred or special place; a crusade or mission.

Powwow: A Native American ceremony or gathering, meaning "spiritual leader," involving singing and dancing, as well as traditional feasting and socialization.

Ritual: A solemn ceremony or rite; an established religious service or observance; prescribed actions.

Sacrifice: The act of giving up or surrendering a person, object, or animal; an offering to a supernatural or divine being.

Secular: A worldly or irreligious interest, specifically focusing on nonspiritual concerns.

Solstice: The longest day of the calendar year and the first day of summer; also the shortest day of the year and the first day of winter; meaning *sol* (the sun) and *stice* (to make stand).

Storytelling: The activity of telling tales, often having social and cultural importance to educate, inform, and preserve traditional values.

Whirling dervish: A Sufi dancer who attends a *tekke* school to receive intensive training to perform the Sema dance; originated in Turkey and inspired by Mevlana Jalaluddin Rumi.

CHAPTER 1 AFRICA

Africa is home to some of the world's most renowned cultural festivals. It is, after all, a continent made up of 54 countries and some 3,000 tribes. Spirituality, rituals, and customs combine with art, music, poetry, storytelling, and dance across beaches, tropical islands, deserts, villages, and historical sites. Here are opportunities to dance the night away.

DANCE THE NIGHT AWAY

In African festivals, dance provides a way to relay historical and cultural events through costumes, masks, body paint, and gestures. The Royal Reed Dance is an annual Swazi and Zulu event that draws 25,000 unmarried and childless girls and women to King Goodwill Zwelithini's royal palace for the eight-day ceremony in South Africa. The colorful event puts on display the women and girls as they sing and dance, adorned with handmade beadwork, in a tribute to the king to ensure his continued power over the Zulu people. It's a display that's graceful and beautiful, but it's also a great honor for the girls and women to be invited to participate in the Royal Reed Dance.

Though some of the more traditional testing requirements, like chastity testing and the age restriction associated with traditional dancing now draw criticism, the festival is a cultural celebration that pays tribute to Zulu origin stories, while educating the participants about appropriate behavior in the culture. The Royal

Women prepare for the Royal Reed Dance.

Women carry their reeds during a procession following the chief princess.

Reed Dance also reinforces a sense of solidarity among the female dancers, as they work together to perform for royalty and spectators.

It's a time of celebration for the rite of passage to womanhood, as they select reeds (which is why it's called a reed dance) and form a procession behind the chief princess. In Zulu mythology, the ancestors came from a reed bed, so the entire display is of enormous significance as a symbolic representation of nature's power. The reed selection also has an additional cultural factor since in mythic terms, the reed remains intact only if the dancer is chaste. The dramatic effect is intense. Imagine the embarrassment if the reed were to break, indicating lost innocence, because the Zulu princess is the first one to select the reed and the one to lay the reed at the king's feet. The entertainment continues until the king joins the dancing.

BUSHFIRE AND OTHER MUSIC FESTIVALS

The MTN Bushfire is an internationally renowned music festival that draws more than 20,000 attendees to the Malkerns Valley, Eswatini (formerly Swaziland). First convened in 2006, the three-day event celebrates creativity with a profusion of world music mixed with artistic expression, including dance, art exhibits, poetry and storytelling, film, and workshops. Although it was first hosted on a family-run sugarcane farm, the activities have far exceeded the initial expectations of the organizers.

Other major music events in Africa include the Fez Festival of World Sacred Music, which was founded in 1994 by Faouzi Skali, a scholar and philanthropist. Located in Morocco, above the Atlas Mountains, the 10-day spiritual celebration draws more than 2 million attendees. With Fes el Bali positioned as a UNESCO World Heritage site, the festival has a unifying influence through interfaith exchange and tolerance. It's a pilgrimage that some attendees make every year to experience dancing monks, Sufi chants, Japanese drummers, Berber music, and whirling dervishes.

Although controversial, the Moroccan Mawazine festival includes some of the world's most famous performance artists. Recent festival performers have included Bruno Mars (pictured), Rihanna, Lenny Kravitz, Jennifer Lopez, and others.

The scenic Lake Malawi serves as the perfect backdrop to the Lake of Stars Festival.

Whereas the Bushfire draws religious fervency, the Mawazine Festival is often a center of controversy. First launched in 2001, Mawazine is one of the most important Moroccan festivals, held in Rabat, Morocco. It is also one of the largest international music festivals, with more than 2 million people drawn to the world-class entertainment. Although it has been applauded for promoting Moroccan culture, diversity, and tolerance, the event is repeatedly the center of controversy because of some of the more risqué musical acts that appear. Wardrobe malfunctions, controversial lyrics, or any other potentially inappropriate onstage behaviors are viewed as inconsistent with the morality restrictions in the country. Critics have also pointed to security and safety concerns, with specific reference to the 2009 festival when a stampede, which killed 11 people, occurred among spectators leaving one of the venues.

The spectacular beauty of Africa is also on display during the Lake of Stars Festival, which attracts 4,000 attendees to Lake Malawi, one of the largest lakes in Africa. First celebrated in 2004, this is an annual international three-day event with a central focus on music and culture. It was first established by Will Jameson to promote tourism, under the influence of the internationally acclaimed festivals World of Music, Arts, and Dance (WOMAD) and Glastonbury. Set against such a scenic backdrop (it's one of the most beautiful places in the world), the festival is a great opportunity for volunteering and collaboration, which expands beyond the festival organizational structure and into the community with activities at orphanages and also through a series of events in Europe and Africa. The Lake of the Stars Festival features an eclectic mix of drama, inspiring talks, and international music performances. Beyond the obvious economic and cultural incentives for launching the festival, it's a great way to shed light on Malawi art while encouraging an international exchange of artistic expression.

FEASTS AND EPIPHANY

Ethiopia's Timkat is the Feast of Epiphany, celebrating the baptism of Jesus by John the Baptist in the Jordan River. It's one of the biggest religious festivals in Ethiopia, and it's also a time of new beginnings. Gondor hosts the largest of the Timkat festivals, with more than 200,000 pilgrims attending. Priests and deacons dress in silk robes, carry umbrellas, dance, and sing as they lead the procession. Participants dress in white while carrying the Tabot, a cloth-wrapped replica of the Ark of the Covenant (that held the Ten Commandments) in procession. Men spend time in prayer and chanting, the water is blessed, and then everyone dives into the frigid water for a symbolic baptism. The festival culminates with the Timkat feast, with flatbread, doro wat chicken, stews, and curries being served.

Meskel is the first big festival of the New Year but also the second most important event (after Timkat) in Ethiopia. The mass blooming of meskel, or yellow daisies, coincides with the time of the festival, so the people bundle them together, tie them to branches, and even set them ablaze. The festival once again celebrates the role of religion, and it takes place in Addis Ababa. Beyond the religious significance, though, it's also a time for Ethiopians to return to their villages to celebrate the national holiday. It was cited as an "Intangible Cultural Heritage of Humanity" by the United Nations Educational, Scientific, and Cultural Organization (UNESCO) for promoting diversity, unity, and integration.

Priests chanting prayers during the Timkat Feast of Epiphany.

A large bonfire, called the Demera, is believed to cancel out sins. It is lit during the Meskel.

First celebrated 1,600 years ago, Meskel commemorates the discovery of Jesus Christ's crucifixion cross by Queen Helena, or Eleni (i.e., St. Helena, mother of Constantine the Great), in the fourth century. The queen followed the direction of a dream to light a bonfire, which showed her where the cross was buried. In commemoration of that discovery, a procession takes place the evening before the festival, culminating with the lighting of a large bonfire, the Demera, which is believed to cancel out sins. A downpour of rain, which is heavy enough to put the bonfire out, signals prosperity in the new year. Some of the faithful also believe that the smoke's direction predicts the future. The people collect ashes from the fire and mark themselves with the sign of the cross.

Camel Racing

Camel racing has ancient origins, but it is still a sporting event in Sudan, India, Kenya, Egypt, and even Australia. Riders revisit cultural traditions with colorful costumes and ancient rituals. Camels were domesticated more than 3,500 years ago, but they have fallen on hard times. They're just not as frequently used now as other, more convenient means of transport exist. Beyond the curiosity factor, camel racing brings back a sense of ancient comradery with the beast, as well as competition, and it continues to be a popular attraction not only in Africa but also in the Middle East and beyond.

FESTIVAL OF THE SAHARA

The Festival of the Sahara, or Camel Festival, is an annual international arts festival. Founded in 1910, it takes place at the edge of the desert, at the oasis in Douz, Tunisia. Along with inspiring and spectacular artistic celebrations, the animal fights and races (yes, camel fights, Arabian horse and greyhound races, and even rabbit chases) offer entertainment of a more sporting variety. The event was first established to promote nomadic culture and traditions when Tunisia was under French rule, but it was modernized under the direction of Habib Bourguiba, who was a prominent Tunisian leader as both prime minister and later as the first president, from 1956 to 1987. The four-day festival has convened every year in December to revisit the nomadic way of life in the Sahara. It's now the oldest and best-known festival in Tunisia.

Tunisians ride camels during the Festival of the Sahara.

The Festival of the Sahara takes attendees out of the everyday into the realm of magic, with galloping Arabian horses, dancing, mesmerizing music, a Bedouin marriage, singing, and poetry recitations (the poetry contest is overseen by the poet Abdellatif Belgacem). Berber women and girls kneel in the sand to perform their "hair dance," tossing their long hair back and forth in an exotic and mesmerizing fashion. Belly dancers, acrobats, and jugglers entertain the crowds, who take part in the traditional reenactments. Ever-popular sand skiing and hot-air balloon rides round out the list of activities. The festival also takes place concurrently with the date harvest, so the traditional foods and crafts sold at the local market become part of the immersive cultural experience.

NIGER'S CURE SALÉE

The Cure Salée, or Festival of the Nomads, is an annual event in Niger marking the end of the rainy season, but it also has important social and cultural significance with its costumed courtship rituals. In keeping with tradition, the Tuareg clans gather at the salt flats for what would be a southward journey. The Tuareg camel parade marks the beginning of the official three-day event, which draws more than 50,000 attendees. It's also a time of dancing, music, storytelling, and artistry.

The Gerewol is a beauty pageant and courtship ritual that takes place as part of the Cure Salée, with a market, clan meetings, and a large festival. Men dress in ceremonial costumes and elaborate makeup as part of their song and dance acts, aimed at winning the favor of the female judges. It's all about stamina, but they must also fit into the traditional conception of attractiveness. To keep up the public display for so many days, the men consume a drink made from fermented bark, which gives them energy and also has hallucinogenic, mind-altering effects.

During Niger's Festival of the Nomads, a beauty pageant called the Gerewol takes place.

SMELL THE BREEZE

Sham el-Nessim (Smelling the Breeze) is an Egyptian national festival to celebrate spring. The event morphed from the ancient Shemu festival, which involved offering green onions, lettuce, and salted fish to Egyptian deities. The festival is now celebrated after the Christian Coptic Orthodox Church Easter holiday every year, although it's also become a secular event. Participants enjoy green, grassy spaces like parks, zoos, and gardens, with their picnic baskets in tow. But it's also a time of coloring and eating eggs, which places the festival in line with other traditional Easter and spring festivals around the world.

The Oshtoora Music Festival in Ras Sidr, Egypt, also takes place at Easter, although it was launched as an arts and music event. Oshtoora is an experiment in participation and collaborative community, designed as a mobile, tent-based camping collective. Inspired by nature, musicians and artists interact with the audience to create sights and sounds that shape the event village. The festival is designed around a cashless, sustainable philosophy that encourages self-expression and global consciousness. The festival is also located at a different site every year, which encourages a freewheeling and spirited experience.

Families gather at a park by the Nile River to celebrate Sham el-Nessim.

BLOOMING FESTIVAL

The Jacaranda Festival is an annual event in Pretoria, which is also called Jacaranda City. It's a celebration of the blooming season for jacaranda trees, which are all (hopefully) on display with their purplish hue. First transplanted from Brazil in the nineteenth century, the 70,000 trees create a gorgeous

The Jacaranda Festival arrives with beautiful blooming purple jacaranda trees.

spectacle. The festival was first established to inspire an influx of tourists as well as breathe life into the city. The effort succeeded beyond expectations, utilizing internationally renowned musical acts, flea markets, and other activities. The very oldest tree in the city (the first one planted) is on the corner of Eastwood and Stanza Bopape, but the whole area along Bosman and Cilliers Streets holds special significance. Locals believe that the blossoms bring good luck, particularly when they fall and land in your hair.

AfrikaBurn focuses on music, performance, and art.

AFRICA'S BURNING MAN

AfrikaBurn is a costumed extravaganza first launched in 2007 in Tankwa, Karoo, South Africa. The focus is on music, performance, and art, but there's an entire philosophical framework behind this "burning man" event. Afrika-Burn joins other alternative cultural festivals around the world in celebrating inclusion and accessibility, with theme camps designed to welcome participants to a commonality of experience. Decommodification, or sustainable consumption, is key to the event's culture and history. It's all about giving without any expectation of repayment. Volunteers are the driving force behind the event, and no branding or advertising is allowed. Beyond the main event, the AfrikaBurn community is active with project planning, as well as social, artistic, and environmental initiatives throughout the year. The Decompression and Streetopia events also extend the AfrikaBurn experience to Cape Town.

TRANSFORMING MASKS

Arts Alive is a month-long international festival in Johannesburg that was first established in 1996. The four-day event celebrates the beginning of spring, and it features dance, arts, poetry, literature, theater, puppetry, and exhibits. The eclectic mix of musical genres includes jazz, hip-hop, Afrobeat, house, and dancehall reggae. Arts Alive also focuses on events that promote creativity and cultural expression for the youth of the country, and the aim is to continually rejuvenate the music and arts scene in Johannesburg.

A masked dancer performs at FESTIMA.

The Festival International des Masques et des Arts (International Festival of Masks and the Arts), or FESTIMA, celebrates traditional African masks for seven days during even years in Dédougou, Burkina Faso. Founded by the Association for the Protection of Masks (ASAMA) in 1996, the festival is designed to promote traditional mask practices. The masks are crafted from wood, textiles, leaves, and straw. The festival represents Togo, Mali, Senegal, and the Ivory Coast, and it draws more than 100,000 people to watch dancers don their masks and perform with accompaniment by whistles and hand drums. In the ceremony, the masked dancer symbolically transforms into a spirit and is able to converse with the ancestors. Translators can then share messages and meaning.

A March for Peace, held on Boganda Day, to celebrate the anniversary of independence.

BOGANDA DAY

Barthélemy Boganda (1910–1959) was a hero and father of the Central African Republic (CAR) and thus is commemorated on the anniversary of his death, March 29. His parents were subsistence farmers, but he was adopted and educated by Catholic missionaries when his parents died. He became the first African Roman Catholic priest from Oubangui-Chari, served missions during World War II, and then entered politics with an anti-racism and anti-colonial platform. He founded the Movement for the Social Evolution of Black Africa (Mouvement pour l'évolution sociale de l'Afrique noire, or MESAN) but also became the first prime minister of the CAR and drafted the constitution. He died under suspicious circumstances in a flaming plane crash on March 29, 1959, but his dream of official independence from France was realized in 1960.

CHAPTER 2 ASIA

Asian festivals offer a unique opportunity to participate in celebrations infused with a wild cacophony of music, parades, delicacies, and fireworks. It's not all fun, food, and costumes, though. Honoring the past is also key to the overall sense of commemoration and reverence, particularly for one's ancestors.

RITUALS FOR HUNGRY GHOSTS AND FUN FOR THE LIVING

Tomb Sweeping Day is a time for families to honor their ancestors. In addition to tidying up the grave, family will come together and bring offerings of food and other gifts.

Beloved ancestors may be long gone, but they aren't forgotten in Asian culture. Respect for, and even worship of, the dead is fundamental to many Asian ethnicities. They may have started as simple funeral or home-altar rituals, but these traditional rites have grown much more elaborate in Asian memorial festivals, such as Tomb Sweeping Day, which is observed in China, Taiwan, Hong Kong, and Chinese cultural communities around the world.

Tomb Sweeping Day is just what it sounds like: a day to clean the family grave. But it's a lot more than just tidying up. It's a time to meditate, honor one's ancestors, and come together as a family and community with a mass migration to wherever "home" is. It's also a time to appease the hungry ghosts with offerings of food and gifts, both on home altars and in temples. It's believed that it is best to keep the wandering spirits happy so that they do not become

Dancers at the Bon Odori Festival in Tokyo.

angry and offended and cause harm to the living. Of course, the connection with ghosts and curses has a way of rekindling people's delight in all sorts of superstitions. Because of this, Tomb Sweeping Day is a popular time for ghost stories, legends, and scary pranks. Add to that the full-moon experience, and you've got an entertainment factor that can entice even the most stoic nonbeliever.

Festivals honoring the dead appear in various forms around the world, but no other region has as many as Asia. Instead of such a strict focus on honoring the dead, events like the Bon Festival (Japan) draw upon the 500-year-old tradition of a return to the ancestral home and the cleaning of the graves, but the Bon Odori folk dance is also an expression of joy and happiness. The dance can be traced to the Odori Nembutsu, a Buddhist dance and chant first intended to make religion more accessible to children. The dance was popularized and secularized in the 1600s, but it was then banned and suppressed for encouraging immorality and inappropriate behavior in the young. The ban was eventually lifted, and the practice spread around the world like wildfire. Now, the Koenji Awa-Odori draws more than 10,000 dancers and more than a million people to Tokyo for one of the biggest street festivals.

INDIA'S HOLI: REJOICE AND "LET LOOSE"

Families gather to light the bonfire that commemorates the defeat of evil.

The most popular legend behind the two-day Indian festival of Holi is a tale of good versus evil, with some horror story elements thrown in. According to the legend, the young prince Prahlada was so devoted to the Hindu god Vishnu that he refused the demands of his demonic father, the king, to worship him instead of the god. His steadfast dedication was rewarded when he was thrown on a bonfire, because his god protected him from the flames. The festival has now moved beyond the good-versus-evil moralization, just as it has moved beyond its origin as a Hindu event in India and Nepal, where it is celebrated by non-Hindus as well. But the burning pyre or bonfire that commemorates the defeat of evil is still part of the celebration. The bonfire evening's events include rituals and prayers for deliverance from the evil within.

The morning after the bonfires, known as Rangwali Holi, is a

Revelers gather in the streets of India, drenched in water and covered by a colored powder known as gulal.

celebration of love and joy, which ties in with a second Holi legend about the Hindi goddess Radha and the god Krishna. This part of the celebration is wild. It's freeing, and it's a profusion of color, fun, and happiness in celebration of spring and rejuvenation. In keeping with the legend in which Krishna and Radha playfully (perhaps as a prank) or lovingly painted each other to make their skin the same color, lovers cover themselves in the same color of paint. Festival-goers are also drenched in water and covered by *gulal*, a colored powder, as part of the boisterous celebration.

Originally, the color was naturally derived from the tesu tree, but the powdered color and paint are now more frequently artificial. The color can last for days on the skin, and clothing is often discarded afterward. It's messy, and it may even be a nuisance, but it's also socially significant. At least in theory, the event celebrates a completely level playing field, with a breaking down of the barriers of class and gender. Perhaps because of the day's association with love and sharing, Holi is sometimes compared with Valentine's Day. Although there's quite a difference in how couples demonstrate their love for one another, both days encourage the free expression of love and emotion.

NOWRUZ: PERSIAN NEW YEAR

The Persian New Year, known as Nowruz (meaning "new day") or Navruz, cele-brates spring and nature awakening. It always begins on the vernal equinox, the first day of spring. The overarching idea behind the holiday is "out with the old, in with the new." In the days leading up the festival, people are busy cleaning their homes and shopping and cooking for family and community parties. An abundance of special foods and sweets is part of every Nowruz celebration. The act of stirring the *sumalak*, made from germinated wheat, is a communal effort. Women sing as they stir the concoction all night, and then they pass it out in the morning. With the first taste, the people make a wish. It's a special, magical time, because day and night are equal, but it's also a reunion and celebration with family, friends, and neighbors.

The 3,000-year-old tradition's historical and cultural significance was recog-nized by the UN General Assembly in 2010 with an International Day of Nowruz. It historically started in Khorasan, parts of which are now geographically located in

Women stir the sumalak *during the celebration of Nowruz.*

Turkmenistan, Iran, Uzbekistan, and Iran, which were part of the ancient Persian Empire (Persia is modern-day Iran). Uzbekistan has its own unique traditions of horse racing and cockfights. But the festival shares some similarities with other familiar holidays. For instance, decorated eggs are reminiscent of Easter, and the use of candles and mirrors to welcome visitors or foresee the future are not unlike some Christmas traditions.

Even with its religious roots for Zoroastrians, Nowruz has become an ever-more-popular secular holiday and community event. Although the festival's rituals are ancient, recent history also makes the celebrations more poignant: Nowruz was banned by the Communists and was rein-stated as a holiday in Uzbekistan only in 1990. It continues to evolve as a cross-cultural celebration of accep-tance and diversity.

Nowruz, like Easter, has a tradition of decorating eggs. These super-sized eggs provide a festive public display.

The Sport of Goat Dragging

It's called *buzkashi* (or *kokpar*) in Central Asia, including in Afghanistan, northern Pakistan, India, Kazakhstan, Uzbekistan, Kyrgyzstan, and Tajikistan, and it's a big part of Nowruz celebrations in these countries. Compared to similar games on horseback, such as polo, it might appear barbaric. After all, what other sport revolves around the fresh carcass of a goat? The challenge is for the mounted players to get a headless goat carcass into a goal. It's definitely a stretch for modern Western sensibilities. There's no doubt, though, that it's a serious sport, dating back to at least the thirteenth century and the rule of Genghis Khan. Although it is traditionally a celebratory event, in recent years it has become more professional, complete with padding and gear to protect riders from the aggressive charges of the opposing team. Still, serious injury is common, and the game can go on for days.

LANTERN LAUNCH AT THE FULL MOON

Lantern festivals, originally part of the traditional rites to commemorate ancestors throughout Asia, have evolved into popular public events. In Cambodia, Thailand, and Laos, for instance, Loi Krathong features the release of *krathong*, or small floating containers with candles (and even money), out into waterways to honor the water spirits and the water goddess, Mae Khongkha. It takes place under the full moon, and each candle has an association with the memory of a loved one, a fervent wish, or a prayer of thankfulness and repentance—for overuse or contamination. The festival of lights has its origins in Sukhothai, an ancient city north of Bangkok, and it celebrates the end to the deluge of rain.

In keeping with the celebratory nature of these events, the Lantern Festival in Taiwan centers on exploding fireworks—the noise is supposed to scare away evil spirits. The floating lanterns are not only beautiful but also lucky. If the spirits are honored and evil spirits warded off, they may fulfill your wishes. That incentive launches a lot of lanterns—so many that a gigantic mess is the inevitable result, with clogged waterways the morning after the full moon.

People launch krathong *into the sky during Loi Krathong in Thailand.*

LIGHT UP THE NIGHT: DIWALI

Diwali (or Divali) is one of the most popular Hindu festivals. The name is derived from *dipavali*, meaning "row or series of lights." Celebrated in India, Nepal, and Hindu communities around the world, the five-day event commemorates, among other things, the triumph of good over evil. Specifically, Hindus remember Lord Krishna's defeat of the demon Narakaasura. Diwali also honors Lakshmi, the goddess of wealth.

A sacrifice, known as *Shakamedhah*, on this day is said to ensure victory. The festival also celebrates the birthday of Matsya (the god Vishnu in the form or incarnation of a fish), as well as the birthday of Vrinda, the god of war. More than 200,000 people gather for the Pushkar Fair and parade, where they participate in ritual bathing, offering food to the gods, and lighting and releasing thousands of earthen lamps. House cleaning, shopping, cooking, and decorating of homes are designed to entice the goddess Lakshmi to enter the house and bestow wealth and happiness upon the family in the coming year. With so much possible good luck and success in the air, Diwali is traditionally the best time to launch a new business to ensure its success. Fireworks, prayer, family feasts, and an abundance of treats punctuate the festivities.

Hindu men and women create a display with hundreds of candles in celebration of Diwali.

MONKS MEDITATE DURING THE RAINY SEASON

The Rain Retreat, or Vassa, is a time of secluded meditation for Theravada Buddhist monks in Laos, Cambodia, Thailand, and Myanmar (formerly Burma). During the monsoon season, comprising three months of heavy rains, the monks remain in the monasteries or within the temple grounds for quiet contemplation. The bonus here is that the thousands of wandering monks stay inside, protecting vulnerable and newly sprouting crops from being trampled.

Many lay people, in sympathy with the monks' reclusive sacrifice, give up bad habits and strive to adopt healthier lifestyles (think not eating meat, avoiding alcohol, quitting smoking). Partly because of this focus on sacrifice, it's often called the Buddhist Lent—reminiscent of the Christian Lent observance, though the Buddhist tradition is some 300 years older. The long period of quiet confinement ends with the Kathina festival, when the community offers up gifts to the monks in appreciation for their sacrifice.

Locals participate in the Kathina festival, giving gifts to the monks in appreciation for their sacrifice.

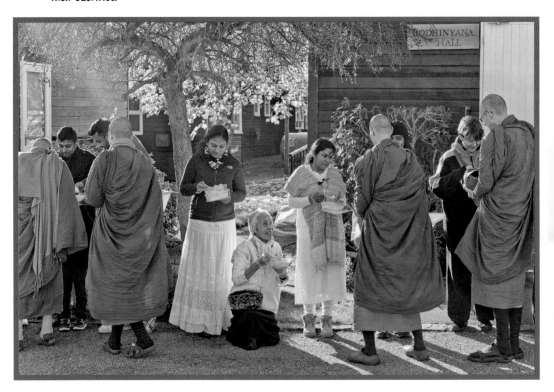

WATCHING THE CHERRY TREES BLOOM IN JAPAN

Japan's hugely popular Cherry Blossom Festival celebrates a time of fleeting beauty when the *sakura* (cherry blossoms) are fully open, over a period of about two weeks in March or April. Because the festival revolves around the blooming season, the date is different every year. The fragility of the cherry blossoms represents the transient,

Japan's Cherry Blossom Festival is one of the most important festivals of the year. Thousands come to see the flowers bloom and celebrate by dancing, singing, and eating lots of food.

perishable nature of life. Flower watching of all kinds (not just cherry blossoms) is so important in Japanese culture that they have a special word for it: *hanami*. But the blooming of the cherry trees is in a class by itself, with dancing, singing, food, and games all part of the festivities. The brief but beautiful blooming of the cherry tree is cause for celebration throughout the country.

Vietnam's lunar New Year is celebrated with parades and dragon dances.

TET NGUYEN IS VIETNAM'S LUNAR NEW YEAR'S PARTY

Tet Nguyen, the biggest party of the year in Vietnam, celebrates the lunar New Year (the first full moon of the year). There's a lot of preparation before the main event, such as cleaning house, cooking special foods, and buying new clothes for everyone. And to start the new year off right, the ancestors must be honored with food, wine, and the burning of incense. Family and community are central to the celebrations, with dancers in dragon costumes, firework displays, and children eagerly awaiting special red envelopes with lucky money inside. It's a time to forget one's troubles and hardships and get ready for the coming year, which will hopefully be a lucky one.

MUCKING AROUND IN SOUTH KOREA'S MUD FESTIVAL

The Boryeong Mud Festival, or Mudfest, has become the most popular (and muddiest) international event in South Korea, with more than 2.2 million visitors at-

Festivalgoers dive into pools of mud at the South Korean Boryeong Mud Festival.

tending the annual summer celebration. Far from being an ancient celebration, the down-and-dirty spring-break party was conceived as a marketing campaign by Boryeong Mud, a cosmetics company, in 1998. It took off with live music, food, and nonstop parties on the beach. Mud is trucked in from the region's flats to support the wild assortment of mud-related events, including wrestling, sliding, a "training" obstacle course, inflatable playgrounds, and giant "mud mega tub" baths. Fireworks and live music on the final night of the two-week party leave everyone looking forward to the next year's Mudfest.

Thousands of festivalgoers enjoy Borneo's Rainforest World Music Festival each year. The festival brings a variety of musical genres and ethnomusical lectures to the stage, making it a much different experience than other music festivals.

THE RAINFOREST WORLD MUSIC FESTIVAL

First convened in 2005, Borneo's Rainforest World Music Festival is recognized as one of the best international music festivals in the world, with 20,000 people in attendance. This world music phenomenon blends traditional and more modern instruments with a variety of musical genres to create a cultural experience infused with Malaysian flavors. Beyond the jams and the delicacies available, there's also a range of ethnomusical lectures and workshops to ensure a full immersive experience. With so much music, food, and hawking of wares, the event has been compared to a local-fair–like bazaar, but it's difficult for any event to compete with the lush jungle backdrop of Borneo. It's a gorgeous, nature lover's paradise, even without the musical extravaganza.

CHAPTER 3 EUROPE

European festivals tap into the history and religious fervor of the countries in that part of the world—with running bulls, parade floats, elaborate costumes, and treasure hunts, among many other events and surprises. Intermingled with the saints and sinners are events that recognize king and country.

BULLS, DEVILS, CHEESE, AND KNIGHTS

The Running of the Bulls is part of the nine-day San Fermín Festival held in Pamplona, Spain. The event involves six to ten bulls, which are released in a cordoned-off part of the city as human participants run out ahead of the bulls, trying to stay safe. According to tradition, the bull run began in the fourteenth century to expedite delivery of the bulls from the fields to the bullring, where they were used in bullfights. The event continues to be controversial, though, mainly because of the number of people who are seriously injured every year. Bull-running events also convene in France, Portugal, and even Mexico, but the events differ from each other in various ways. In the Toros en el Mar, held in Dénia, Spain, for example, the bulls run into the sea.

Spain's El Colacho (Baby-Jumping) Festival involves a person dressed as a devil jumping over recently born babies to cleanse their original sin, passed down to them because of Adam and Eve's disobedience in the Garden of Eden, according to Christian beliefs. The event has probably been around since the 1600s. Beyond the religious aspect, the festival is also a historical and cultural

Participants run ahead of bulls at the nine-day Running of the Bulls Festival.

tradition. Rose petals shower down on the babies, freshly relieved of their "sin," while priests bless them, and parents gather them up. Church officials discourage the practice of El Colacho because they say it isn't in sync with religious teachings, but it's still as popular as ever.

Instead of jumping over babies, Cooper's Hill Cheese-Rolling and Wake is an annual event held in England that involves releasing and rolling a round of Double Gloucester cheese down the hill. The goal of the mad dash is to catch the cheese as it plummets down Cooper's Hill. The round can reach 70 miles per hour (112.7 kph) so the reality is that the first person to make it across the finish line wins. The prize, unfortunately, is just the cheese. The origins of the event may have involved grazing rights, or it may have been an ancient ritual where burning brushwood bundles were rolled to symbolize the coming of spring. Whatever the origin of the event, it has been the center

Hundreds of people take part in the Cooper's Hill Cheese-Rolling and Wake in England. The hill is quite steep so rather than run down, many end up rolling, just like the wheel of cheese.

of mounting debate over public safety and crowd control concerns. Every year, at least one person is carted off in an ambulance, but the attendees and organizers still insist on putting on the dangerous footrace.

To round out this collection of festivals, the Palio di Siena is a biannual festival in Siena, Italy, that features medieval costumes and armor, a flag ceremony, singing, the blessing of horses, a procession, and a competitive horse race. The rituals originated in the fourteenth century and focus on the competition between the city's regions.

MASKS AND MUSIC

Sechseläuten (also referred to as *Sächsilüüte* in the local dialect), or Six o'Clock Chimes, is a Swiss festival to celebrate spring in Zürich. In the tradition of Burning Man, Sechseläuten culminates with the burning of winter, represented by Böögg, a snowman figure who is linked to Carnival season. Historically, work ceased at sundown during the winter, but upon the chiming of the six o'clock bells in the summer, Sechseläuten ushered in a time of daylight "free" hours. The festival also features traditional costumes, floats, ceremonial horses, and, of course, food and drink.

Cornwall, England's Masked Ball is a biannual event in the summer and fall at the Los Flambardos Theme Park. First convened in 2006, the festival is now one of the biggest Halloween parties in Europe, complete with voodoo influences. Partygoers dance, sing, and chant the night away dressed as psycho killers, skeletons, and voodoo characters. In continuation of the ultimate party theme, the Glastonbury Festival of Performing Arts is held near Pilton, Somerset, UK. The festival was launched in 1970 by Michael Eavis, who was inspired by

The Sechseläuten snowman is burned, representing the destruction of winter.

Bubblemen and women create a display of giant bubbles for children at the Green Man festival.

free-festival and counterculture movements. With more than 175,000 attendees, the event features music, art, comedy, circus, and cabaret.

Green Man is a four-day outdoor arts-and-music festival held in Brecon Beacons, Wales. The event was established in 2003, and it now draws 20,000 attendees to see 1,500 music performances across 17 stages, as well as live comedy, theater, poetry, and literature. In myth and legend, the Green Man symbolizes rebirth and the cycle of growth, often consisting of leaves, but he's also linked to the Oak King, Pan, and Robin Hood, as well as many other outlaws and heroes through literature and history. The Green Man festival also taps into counterculture by focusing on local suppliers, no corporate sponsors, sustainability, and high-quality music. Every year, the festival culminates by setting the iconic "Green Man" wicker structure ablaze.

BATTLES OF THE ORANGES AND TOMATOES

The Battle of the Oranges, or the Carnival of the Oranges, is an Italian festival in Ivrea that involves three days of orange throwing. It's the largest food fight in Italy, although the origins of the twelfth-century skirmish are a matter of some contention. One story places the focus on a tyrant, Marquis Raineri di Biandrate, who attacked a young, soon-to-be-married miller's daughter, Violetta. She fought back, drew her dagger, and beheaded her attacker. Inspired by her bravery, the people of Ivrea stormed the castle in all-out civil war and burned it to the ground.

   The carnival commemorates the young girl's bravery, as the designated *mugnaia* (miller's daughter) travels in procession through the streets, distributing sweets and presents to the crowd. The nine civil Aranceri squads (or orange-thrower teams) are led by a "general," and they all dress in battle attire to represent the rebellious people rising up against the tyrannical nobles. Altogether, they hurl some 500,000 pounds of oranges. Against the backdrop of such volatile historical events, the Battle of the Oranges also features floats, elaborate battle-gear costumes, and live music. In the end, one of the generals claims victory, but few of the participants

Masked people are protected by traditional helmets while throwing oranges at Ivrea's Battle of the Oranges.

leave the field of battling oranges unscathed (without bruises, cuts, or wounded pride).

The Battle of the Tomato (La Tomatina) is held in Buñol, Spain, every year. The first such event was held in 1945. As the name suggests, it involves people throwing tomatoes at each other in another huge food fight (even bigger than the Battle of the Oranges). Although the first tomato battle was something of

Buñol, Spain, holds one of the largest food fights. Every year, hundreds gather to participate in the Battle of the Tomato.

an unforeseen accident, subsequent events continued to be planned, despite the best efforts of the police to suppress and break up the staged food fights. The police and city officials even went so far as to cancel the event in the 1950s, but there was so much backlash, with protests and mock tomato burials, that the fans finally succeeded in gaining official recognition for their event.

What Are the Origins of the Mask?

Masks appear as part of ceremonies and celebrations around the world, but they also offer important insight into a culture's customs and practices. They are typically meant to be worn on the face, as a disguise, protection, ornamentation, or ceremonial representation, but some masks are designed to cover the entire body. Masks can also be used for celebratory, religious, or even therapeutic purposes. Adam and Eve's guilty fig-leaf coverings in the Garden of Eden may be the very earliest forms of masks, but other depictions in Paleolithic cave drawings also demonstrate various masks with the cultural significance associated with the facial coverings.

Masks are of particular importance in festivals and celebrations because they can hide a person's identity but also allow for free-spirited play or dramatic performances, gender ambiguity or role reversal, and revolutionary class-busting. In the most extreme personifications, masks allow for extreme behavior, including scanty or no clothing, free love, frenzied rites, sacrifice, and violence. Historically, the controversial festivals of Bacchus, the Roman god of wine and fertility, led to the arrest and execution of some 7,000 cult leaders. In other traditions, though, masks support the supernatural transference of power and spirit in culturally positive (good) or malignant (evil) ways. Masks and facial coverings are also associated with secret societies and subversive movements.

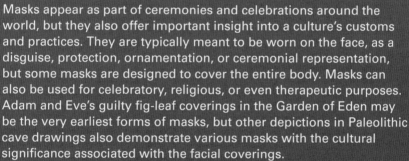

UNMASKING THE TRICKERY

Carnival is the ultimate celebration, and the series of festivals across Europe makes for a cross-cultural extravaganza that's difficult to miss. With costumes, dancing, food, and games, each location is just one more stage set for wild abandon, partying, and costumed revelry. In Berlin, it's the Carnival of Cultures in June, including a Sunday parade. In Spain, there's the ever-famous Carnival in Cadiz and the Sitges Carnival, but the Las Fallas Fiesta has the lofty designation as the loudest festival, with a conflagration of fireworks, costumes, and lights.

Belgium's Carnival of Binchehas been recognized by UNESCO as a Masterpiece of the Oral and Intangible Heritage of Humanity. But who would miss the Venice Carnival (Carnevale di Venezia), with such a rich history and an enduring culture all its own? This festival began in the eleventh century. But it did not always do well over the centuries, and it was banned by Mussolini in the 1930s. After a long hiatus, it returned in 1979. Beyond the lavish costumes and elaborate parades, the zombie walk might just be the perfect way to bring your entire Carnival adventure to a close.

The Venice Carnival features elaborate costumes and masks.

GRAPES OF MIRTH

The Harol Wine Festival, or San Vino, convenes in Haro, Spain, on June 29 for the Batalla de Vino (Battle of Wine). Yes, there's the Battle of the Oranges and the Battle of the Tomatoes, but this one involves a whole other level of festival participation in the Rioja wine region. Here, the wine fight quickly becomes a huge party, with dancing, music, bar hopping, and a procession of sodden wine bearers. The event also happens to fall on the day of commemoration for the patron saint, San Pedro.

The Fiesta de Cascamorras occurs in Granada, Spain. With more than 20,000 people in attendance every year, it was even named a Festival of National Tourism Interest. While participants don't spray wine on each other, they do cover one another with olive oil, combined with colored paste. It's a glorious mess. According to the stories, Cascamorras, a worker from Guadix, unearthed an image of the Virgen de la Piedad (Our Lady of Mercy). The townspeople of Baza, where he was working, claimed the image for their town. A tentative truce was negotiated, which would have meant that Cascamorras would collect the image and bring it to Guadix for one day each year. Unfortunately, the Baza people refused to honor the deal. They pelted Cascamorras with olive oil, eggs, and flour every year when he attempted to retrieve it.

The Haro Wine Festival is just as fun as it is messy. Festivalgoers not only drink wine but pour it all over each other, making a very big mess.

THE DEVIL'S IN THE HOLIDAYS

Germany's Krampusnacht is one of the more frightening Christmas celebrations.

Krampusnacht, or Krampus Night, is a huge annual celebration in Germany, centering on Krampus, a horned beast or incubus, but also the antithesis of Saint Nicholas, or Santa Claus (who was popularized as early as the eleventh century). Instead of spreading peace, joy, and lots of toys as a jolly old saint, Krampus is a hairy, cloven, and horned creature who punishes bad children. In Germany and Bavaria, men dress up as demons and parade or run through town, while women dress as Frau Perchta, a fertility goddess.

The origins of the festival date back to the sixteenth century via masked devils or animalistic figures that appeared in morality plays, but Krampus also represents the "evil" pagan supernatural in stark comparison with the "good" Saint Nicholas. The devilish Krampus takes to the streets to fill boots with coal or spanking switches, or even to carry off bad children in his wheelbarrow or basket to chain them up and torture them. With parades, costumes reminiscent of a Halloween horror show, and free-spirited debauchery, Krampusnacht is the opposite of traditional, saccharine-like Christmas celebrations.

Scotland's Up Helly Aa fire festival has been an annual event held in the Shetland Islands since the 1880s, with several lapses due to the death of Queen Victoria, World War I, and World War II. Concern for public safety inspired the evolution from the festive tar-barreling (literally setting tar barrels on fire) and mischief-making to a torch-bearing parade, with influences from Viking history. The procession ends when the squads of guizers, or masks, throw their torches into a Viking longship. The costumed participants then perform their skit or act (singing, dancing, or other stagecraft).

KING'S DAY

Koningsdag, or King's Day, is a celebration of spring in the Netherlands. As the name suggests, the national holiday also celebrates the monarch's birth. The name of the celebratory event was changed from Queen's Day to King's Day when King Willem Alexander was crowned. Queen Beatrix abdicated in 2013, making her son the first king since 1890. Nearly a million people turn out for the street-party extravaganza. Partygoers wear orange in honor of the House of Orange but also because orange is the national color. With widespread free markets across the city, Amsterdam becomes one of the world's biggest international flea markets. The city center is open to foot traffic, but public transportation is diverted. Oranjebloesem is just one of the annual parties at Blijburg aan Zee, a city beach.

On Koningsdag, people take to the streets and the canals in Amsterdam.

Bloomsday participants reenact the funeral procession from a chapter out of Ulysses.

IT'S RAINING BOOKS

Bloomsday is an annual celebration in Dublin, Ireland, that celebrates the Irish writer James Joyce's life and works. It's celebrated on June 16, because Joyce's famously controversial novel *Ulysses* is set on that day—it's the day when Leopold Bloom, the main protagonist, meets Nora, the love of his life. The event is also named after Bloom. The event first took place in 1924, but it has evolved and grown over the decades, with more than 60,000 attendees now involved in the Dublin activities and even more fans involved in events around the world in Australia, Canada, the Czech Republic, France, Hungary, Italy, and the United States. The festivities involve theatrics, pub crawls, marathon readings of *Ulysses*, literary tours, and musical events. By dressing as characters from the book, fans immerse themselves in Joyce's world, once again reinforcing the importance of the book to modern sensibilities.

OKTOBERFEST

Oktoberfest takes over Munich, Germany, for 16–18 days from September to October, with music, dancing, Bavarian-costumed parades, poetry, horse races, and flowers all involved. The first event was held in 1810, but the annual celebrations subsequently helped to define the new nation, forging essential connections between the royalty and the people. With more than 6 million people now attending the

Germany's Oktoberfest features Bavarian costumes, large pretzels, and very large glasses of beer.

festivities, Oktoberfest is also famous for offering the earliest amusement park rides and sideshows. That history of innovation and spectacular entertainment has continued and evolved into an ever-more-spectacular extravaganza, making it one of the most famous and largest Volksfest (folk festivals) in the world. Beyond rides like "Skyfall" and "Devil's Wheel," Oktoberfest involves free-flowing beer in 15 beer tents and dozens of food tents to sustain the crowds (some of the tents hold 10,000 people).

The European Balloon Festival takes place on Igualada. It is the largest in Europe with more than 25,000 attendees.

WINTER VENTURES

The European Balloon Festival is the largest event in Spain but also one of the largest in Europe, with more than 25,000 attendees converging on Igualada. The four-day event was founded in 1997, and it's been joined by festivities in Italy, France, Hungary, the Netherlands, Belgium, Spain, Germany, Switzerland, and Sweden. The event is dependent on good weather, of course, so some years are more spectacular.

The World Snow Festival draws international artists to the small glacial village of Grindelwald, Switzerland, for an ice-sculpture extravaganza. The very first event took place in 1982, when Japanese artists carved a giant Heidi statue out of ice. That giant sculpture was a tribute to the Swiss author Johanna Spyri and her ever-popular children's book, *Heidi*, but that first event has grown into a matter of national pride in its celebration of cultural heritage and artistic ingenuity.

CHAPTER 4 LATIN AMERICA AND THE CARIBBEAN

More than almost anywhere in the world, festivals in Latin America and the Caribbean are colorful adventures—full of self-expression, amazing foods and flavors, and an enthusiastic zest for life. The mix of events celebrate the harvest, commemorate the dead, and offer spectacles of ethnic pageantry.

CARNIVAL

The Rio Carnival is one of the most famous festivals in the world, with origins dating to the 1640s. With influences from the Italian Carnevale, the festivities have spread across South America and are celebrated in Argentina, Bolivia, Peru, Uruguay, and elsewhere—including in Trinidad and Tobago. Dating back to the 1640s, the Rio Carnival honored the Greek wine gods with an event that was originally called the Entrudo Festival. The celebration was introduced to Brazil by the Portuguese, but it also melded with religious and African influences.

In a city known for its beautiful beaches and rocking nightlife, the Carnival in Rio de Janeiro offers the biggest bang for a Carnival buck, drawing 2 million people for the proliferation of elaborate costumes, music, and dancing. It really is the biggest (and best) show on earth, with more than 600 street parties erupting around the city. With so much going on in this mega-celebration, one of the key

Rio's Carnival is one of the most famous festivals in the world. It is filled with performances from musicians, singers, and dancers. The massive Sambadrome, shown here, was built especially for the annual celebration.

The Oruro Carnival features some wild and intricate costumes that tell the story of good versus evil.

focal points is still the Samba Parade, which draws top dancers to compete for the championship.

The Rio Carnival offers something for almost everyone, though that also means that it brings a criminal element to the city. Controversies over the lack of fabric in many of the glittery and risqué costumes have also erupted. Likewise, the racially insensitive lyrics in some of the featured performances have been objected to by some.

Oruro Carnival is Bolivia's largest Carnival festival, with 20,000 dancers and 10,000 musicians bedecked in elaborate costumes. It draws more than 400,000 attendees. Catholic rites combine with Uru Uru (Oruro) rituals and traditions to more accurately represent the full cultural flavor of the region, but the Oruro Carnival also tells the story of Spanish occupation, with a side note of a good-versus-evil morality play that's common with religious celebrations.

The miraculous story of the Virgin of Candelaria aiding a fatally wounded thief adds a controversial dimension to the festivities. Critics claim that the Spaniards manipulated the story to convince the people to build a church for the Virgin Mary. The parade offers a stage for the representation of Archangel San Miguel, followed by figures from Uru mythology: bear, condor, monkey, and puma. The costumed representation of Lucifer and his devil women, China Supay, put on a tempestuous dance display.

FESTIVALS OF THE SAINTS

The Festival de la Candelaria is one of the most important and inspiring festivals in South America, which goes on for two weeks in February in Bolivia, Chile, Peru, Uruguay, and Venezuela (second in size to the Rio Carnival). The event draws more than 200 music groups to celebrate the patron saint of the city, the Virgin of Candelaria (one of the figures representing the Virgin Mary), with colorfully costumed-and-masked dancers forming parades as they rhythmically weave around the city. Mirrors and jewels feature prominently in their colorful attire, which also serves to underscore the eclectic mix of religious ritual and pagan tradition.

Of course, the Festival de la Candelaria is not the only event that centers on religion or focuses on a commemoration of the saints. The Fiesta de Santiago de Apóstol is a July event in Puerto Rico that commemorates Saint James the Apostle, with exhibitions, concerts, and theater performances. Lights and colors fill the Plaza del Obradoiro, with multidimensional projections on the cathedral. The event also features dancing, bagpipes, open-air celebrations, and incense burning.

Montserrat's St. Patrick's Day is a day of national celebration, with costumes and partying. Montserrat is called the "Emerald Isle of the Caribbean." Many settlers with Irish heritage escaped to Montserrat, which was a British protectorate

A music group performs during a celebration during the Festival de la Candelaria.

The Virgin of Candelaria is at the center of celebrations in South America.

and haven for the displaced and persecuted (they were sent into exile by the English military leader Oliver Cromwell). The festival is a weeklong event that recollects that painful past and educates the public about those Irish genealogical roots, while acknowledging a failed slave uprising on St. Patrick's Day in 1768. So there's a mix of celebrations with influences from both Irish and African cultures and origins, including a freedom run, masquerade dances, traditional food, and, of course, green beer. Many of the activities also center on the reconstructed slave village.

How Did John Canoe Play a Trickster?

John Canoe was the European name given to a West African tribal chief and folk hero who outsmarted the English in the early eighteenth century. He was an Akan warrior from Axim, Ghana, until he was enslaved and brought to the West Indies. He demanded the right to celebrate with his people, but he was refused. Instead, he took over the Brandenburger Fortress of Fort Fredericksburg and defended it from 1708 until 1724, when he finally gave up the fort and slipped into obscurity. During that time, he supported his private army as well as the local population of Ahanta people. He also traded with all nations, and he made off with enough gems to build himself a mansion. His history and achievements have become legend and are admired by the people as an example of standing up against white conquests. He also represented his own interests, which places him squarely in a trickster role.

JUNKANOO FESTIVAL

A man dances at the Junkanoo festival.

The Junkanoo Festival takes to the streets of the Bahamas, with themed costumes, dancing, and music, during the traditional Christmas holiday season. As variations on the legend would have it, Junkanoo was heavily influenced by the tricksterish activities of John Canoe, a Western African tribal chief, in the early eighteenth century. He's a folk hero who escaped the bonds of slavery when his masters refused to allow him to celebrate with his people. Though the story of John Canoe is typically the most well-known theory for the festival's origin, others say that the name Junkanoo is a translation of *gens inconnus*, which means "unknown" or "masked people." Still others point to similarities with the Igbo Okonko tradition of horned maskers from Southern Nigeria and cite the influences of the Yam Festival in celebration of Njoku Ji, a guardian deity.

Perhaps first and foremost, though, the Junkanoo Festival is also linked to slave celebrations held in honor of the three days they got off for Christmas. Slaves initially covered their face with flour paste in celebration of

Men perform in traditional garb in celebration of Junkanoo.

Boxing Day, but the disguise transitioned to the use of a wire mask on a stick. The tie-ins of the traditional Christmas masquerade of revelry, Igbo Okonko traditions, and the trickster-like antics of John Canoe lessened somewhat with the abolition of slavery. However, the history and tradition of the day have still coalesced into a cultural extravaganza that draws attendees from around the world—with a series of events that extend from Nassau to the Abacos, Bimini, Eleuthera and Harbour Island, and Grand Bahama Island. The festival continues to stand apart for its unique costumes, with crinkly paper glued to fabric, cardboard, aluminum rods, or wood (wires help give the costumes shape), but also in combination with elaborate floats crafted with Styrofoam, crepe, and papier-mâché. The processions, costumes, dancing, and music culminate in judging with prizes handed out for best costumes, group presentation, and best music.

PROCESSIONS OF THE CROSS

Peru's Señor de los Milagros (Lord of Miracles) is not only one of the most important Peruvian religious events but also one of the largest processions in the world. The festival centers around a seventeenth-century depiction of the crucifixion of Jesus Christ, who is pictured on the cross, with the Virgin Mary and Mary Magdalene looking on. An African slave painted the mural, but this unknown artist's work was deemed miraculous after it survived a disastrous earthquake in 1655 (and then again in 1687). The mural became a pilgrimage site after reports of healing began to surface.

Although perhaps not as extraordinarily miraculous, Guatemala's Semana Santa, or Holy Week, is a religious holiday that takes place during the week before Easter. It was first convened in 1524. One of the popular features of the celebration has always been the processions, with religiously themed floats. Participants also wear robes to demonstrate penitence.

Peru's Señor de los Milagros sees several processions of Jesus Christ on the crucifix.

DAY OF THE DEAD

Dia de los Muertos (Day of the Dead) is a Mexican holiday, with influences from indigenous Aztec, Maya, and Toltec cultures. Beyond the history, traditions, and rituals, UNESCO recognized the festival for its Intangible Cultural Heritage of Humanity in 2008. Because death is seen as a natural part of life, this festival originated as a respectful way to keep the memory of loved ones alive, as their spirit returns to walk among them. Over time, the festival evolved, with influences from Christian feasts, harvest celebrations, and other religious rites.

Costumed revelers set up *ofrenda* (offering) altars, which include foods, sugar skulls, toys, and other memorabilia to welcome the dead during the first days of November. Although often linked with the darkness and horror of Halloween, this holiday is really a way to celebrate life, because the cycle of life means that something new will come from death. Everything associated with the rituals and sacrifices of this day are meant to demonstrate deep respect for those loved ones who have passed. Also, the dead would be insulted by sadness or mourning, so participants lay out *cempasúchil* flowers in pathways to lead spirits to their family homes. It's an explosion of vibrant colors with many decorations, including images of monarch butterflies—believed to hold departed spirits. Monarchs are also important to the day (November 1), because that's supposed to be the day when the butterflies arrive in Mexico for the winter.

Mexico's Dia de los Muertos is one of the liveliest celebrations. It is filled with parades and revelers dressed as skeletons and sugar skulls.

FESTIVALS OF SUN AND FLOWERS

Peru's Inti Raymi, or Festival of the Sun, honors the sun god Inti. Traditionally, the event centered on a procession of ancient cloth-wrapped mummies, llama sacrifice, dancing, colorful traditional costumes, and reading coca leaves. The festival celebrates the winter solstice, the coming of the new year, and Inca origins. The modern-day version has been toned down, with no mummy parade and only one sacrifice, compared with the hundreds in ancient times.

The Flower Festival is one of the most important events in Medellín, Colombia. The event was first convened in 1957 in celebration of the success of wildflower export, but the festivities have evolved and grown into an international extravaganza. The 10-day event still centers on flowers, but other features include concerts, art exhibitions, classes, and fairs.

The Crop Over festival is one of the most colorful events in Barbados. The earliest celebrations occurred more than 200 years ago around harvest time at the sugarcane plantations. Revelers dress in elaborate sequined costumes with feathers and jewels. The dusk-till-dawn parties feature arts and crafts, music, dancing, and moving bars.

Farmers pose with a flower display of their creation for Colombia's Flower Festival.

Tango dancers compete during the Tango Festival's main event in hopes of winning the Tango World Cup.

JUST DANCE THE TANGO

The Tango Festival is an annual dance event in Buenos Aires, the birthplace of tango. It's also the world's largest tango fiesta. UNESCO recognized the event as part of the world's Intangible Cultural Heritage of Humanity in 2009. Beyond the competitive dance events, the Tango Festival features a broad spectrum of activities, from films, book readings, and city tours to tango classes (for dancers of every level) and theatrical shows. The main event, though, still is the more than 400 world-renowned dancing couples who dance away in the championship all in the hope of winning the Tango World Cup.

MISTURA

Mistura was first established in 2008 in Lima, Peru, and it quickly became South America's largest food festival. The festival draws more than 400,000 visitors for a diverse, fusion-flavored experience of street-cart vendors and famous chefs,

Musicians dressed in traditional clothing perform for the Mistura festival.

such as Virgilio Martinez. It also taps into the delectable flavors of more than 400 restaurants. The 10-day event takes place in September or October and offers the very best in Peruvian cuisine. The festival is often made part of a full tour and exploration of Peru, with cooking lessons and amazing cultural immersion. The new theme each year is specifically chosen so that it highlights a unique perspective on Peru's amazing cultural heritage, with dances, concerns, food demonstrations, contests, and awards. For example, one year's theme focused on Peru's biodiversity. More than anything, the Mistura festival highlights the immersive melting pot that is the Peruvian experience, with influences from Africa, China, Japan, Spain, and indigenous cultures.

The St. Lucia Jazz Festival features concerts, art shows, and more.

STORYLAND

The Storyland Festival, formerly Summerland Cartagena, is an annual electronic music festival in the beach destination of Santa Marta, Colombia. It's a groundbreaking phenomenon as well as one of the most important festivals in Latin America. With its proximity to the Caribbean coast, participants dance the night away on the sands of Playa Bello Horizonte. The event also prides itself on inclusivity, and it features big names, local talent, and up-and-coming artists. It's a huge tourist draw for Colombia.

Other music festivals include the St. Lucia Jazz Festival, which first convened in 1992 as a stunt to extend the tourist season with local and international music. The event features a mix of educational lectures, street fairs, art shows, and both free and paying concerts. The Reggae Sumfest is the largest annual music festival in Jamaica. The event was first launched in 1993, and it's now extended to a six-day festival in Montego Bay.

CHAPTER 5 MIDDLE EAST

The Middle East is becoming a more diverse region, compared to the ancient practices and ceremonies of these lands, and that evolution is reflected in exciting new developments in the world of festivals, particularly in the music, art, and entertainment at these events. As a result, cultural awareness and sensitivity are now more important than ever.

ROCKING IN LEBANON AND BEYOND

Lebanon offers several popular music festivals, including the Wickerpark Festival, a grassroots alternative festival in Batroun. Beyond the ultra-laid-back feel of this event, participants camp out by the beach at Ô-Glacée. The festival also supports zero waste, outdoor activities, and projects focused on activism, art, and sustainability. The event now inspires 18,000 to attend, along with 80 bands and 150 artists and performers.

The Beirut & Beyond International Music Festival was founded in 2013. The four-day event features concerts, lectures, and debates. It's also the first independent festival to support young musicians from the Middle East.

Crews set the stage for the oldest cultural event in the Hezbollah stronghold. The Baalbek International Festival is held at the Temple of Bacchus.

Cairo's jazz band, The Shakers, performs at the Cairo Jazz Festival.

The Baalbek International Festival is the oldest cultural event in the region. It takes place in a Hezbollah stronghold near the Syrian border. It's also located near the Temple of Bacchus, that famous Roman trickster god of fertility and wine. First convened in 1955, the event is government-sponsored to support Lebanese culture and tourism, and it draws more than 40,000 attendees.

Dubai's Wasla is a music festival that's all about connection, with artists from Algeria, Bahrain, Jordan, and Lebanon—covering everything from electronic music and jazz to pop, reggae, and rock. Finally, the Cairo Jazz Festival is an international event that was founded in 2009 by Amro Salah, a pianist, producer, and composer. It's a three-day celebration that supports cultural exchange, inspires a new generation of musicians, and presents the best jazz from around the world.

RAMADAN

Ramadan is the ninth (and holiest) month of the Islamic calendar, based on the cycles of the moon. It's observed by Muslims around the world as a period of recitation and reading the Qu'ran, five daily prayers, spiritual reflection, and fasting (*sawm*). Ramadan, which means "scorching heat" or "dryness," commemorates the first revelations of the Qu'ran to the Prophet Muhammad in the seventh century. The fasting takes place from sunrise to sunset every day, beginning the morning after the crescent moon can be seen (which has led to controversy and international inconsistencies regarding the best date for Ramadan to begin). Practicing Muslims also avoid drinking alcohol, taking oral medication, smoking, gossiping, lying, fighting, and engaging in any other behaviors that are considered immoral under Islam.

People gather at communal tables to break fast for the iftar meal.

During Ramadan, people take part in giving back to the community. Here, men and women hand out food for the iftar meal.

Ramadan is a time of sacrifice and personal reflection but also a time to focus on forgiveness and generosity (and to recognize and contribute to alleviating hunger around the world). It's also a time for families as well as communities to unite, as they all gather together in celebration, but also commit themselves to one another and to God. In particular, the *iftar* meal, the breaking of the fast at sunset, is often a social gathering.

In some countries, the court prosecutes those who fail to observe Ramadan. Officials arrest those Muslims who smoke or eat in public, but they can also charge those who sell food to Muslims (even if they are non-Muslim). Although some countries enforce the restrictions much more adamantly, prison sentences, flogging, and stiff fines are just a few of the possible punishments. There are, of course, exemptions to the requirements of fasting for those who are ill (either mentally or physically), frail, or traveling, and for women who are pregnant. Even without the actual charges and punishment, that threat and the underlying expectation of repercussions help to reinforce appropriate observances.

FEASTS AND BREAKING FASTS

The Prophet's Birthday, or Mawlid al-Nabi, is the observance of the Prophet Muhammad's birthday in November and is a national holiday in some Muslim-majority countries. The exact date of his birth is unknown, but that's just one of the controversies surrounding the day and the permissibility of the celebrations related to Muhammad's birth. The celebration was first launched by Abu al-Abbas al-Azafi in Sabta—with torch-lit processions, public sermons, feasting, and animal sacrifice—in an effort to bring the Muslim community together, but it has become an important Islamic celebration that is now observed by most denominations around the world. The Prophet's Birthday is a time for lectures, feasting, parades, and other carnival activities. In general, Shia and Sunni scholars allow for the celebration of Mawlid as a way to show love for the Prophet, whereas the Ahmadiyya and Wahhabi sects reject and oppose the celebration as offensive and forbidden.

During the Prophet's Birthday, Muslims gather to listen to lectures.

A procession takes place in honor of the Prophet's birthday.

The Festival of the Breaking of the Fast is celebrated at the conclusion of Ramadan, when the new moon is sighted. It lasts for three days, with a combination of prayer at the mosque, feasting, and shopping. It also involves decorating homes with lights and giving gifts. Muslim women and girls also paint their hands, arms, legs, and feet with temporary henna or *mehndi* tattoos to bring good luck. Finally, the Feast of the Sacrifice lasts for a single day, but it is more important than the Festival of the Breaking of the Fast. As the name suggests, the Feast of Sacrifice is a "solemn festival" that traditionally involves animal sacrifice and prayer to commemorate Abraham (Ibrahim) and his obedience and willingness to sacrifice his only son, Isaac. In keeping with the lamb that was provided to Abraham, the people make a sacrifice and divide the animal in three parts for the needy, home, and relatives.

Why Is Mawlid Controversial?

The Mawlid is celebrated as the birthday of the Prophet Muhammad, the founder of Islam and the last messenger of God. Although it is often seen as a time of parades, feasting, and commemoration, the day (and the celebration) is controversial, not only because the exact date of birth is not known or recorded but also because many other events in the Prophet Muhammad's life are not recognized.

THE MARTYRDOM OF HUSAYN

The Day of Ashura is the 10th day of Muharram in Afghanistan, Azerbaijan, Bahrain, Bangladesh, Iran, Iraq, Lebanon, and Pakistan. For Shia and Sunni Muslims, it's a holy day of mourning and commemoration for Husayn ibn Ali, the grandson of Prophet Muhammad and the fourth caliph (religious and cultural leader). With the death of Muawiyah I, Ali ibn Abi Talib (Muhammad's cousin and son-in-law) and his rebel followers challenged the succession of Yazid, called for a return of leadership under a descendant of the Prophet Muhammad, and named Husayn as the rightful leader. He and his followers also invited Husayn to join them in the refuge of Kufah, which is modern-day Iraq. Meanwhile, Yazid sent troops to restore order and threaten punishment to the rebels. When Husayn and his followers arrived in Kufah (72 strong, with women and children), they were attacked by more than 4,000 men, massacred, and desecrated in the Battle of Karbala. The day is a time of mourning for the martyrdom of Husayn and his family, with passion plays and other reenactments.

Ashura also marks the day when Moses led the Israelites in their escape from Egypt. They fled across the Red Sea on a seafloor path created by divine intervention, which is now often referred to as the Parting of the Red Sea. It's also a remembrance of the day Noah emerged from the ark on top of Mount Arafat, after 40 days and 40 nights of rain. To round out the series of commemorative events associated with Ashura, there's also recognition for the day when the Prophet Muhammad arrived in Medina.

On the Day of Ashura, Afghan Shiites will beat themselves with chains, and even blades, to mark Ashura.

HOLIDAY IN HAIFA

The festivities in Haifa, Israel, offer an eclectic mix of end-of-year holidays—including Christmas, Eid al-Fitr and Eid al-Adha, Hanukkah, and Ramadan. It all culminates in a street party every Friday and Saturday in December. Haifa is the third largest city in Israel, and it's also a port city. Against a backdrop of the Mediterranean Sea and the Bahá'í Gardens, the festival features performers, food stalls, and outdoor exhibits, located mostly in the Wadi Nisnas neighborhood.

For an even deeper spiritual experience while in Haifa, the Stella Maris Carmelite Monastery, built in 1836, is famous not only for its frescos of St. Elijah but also for the tomb of 200 French soldiers who were left in a hospital on this site by Napoleon in 1799 and subsequently killed by Ottoman forces. The Haifa cable car also offers an amazing tour of the landscape from high up on the way to the monastery. The panoramic views are just part of it, though. The cultural and historical significance of the place, including Elijah's Cave, draws Christian, Jewish, and Muslim pilgrims for memorialization, meditation, and prayer. It's one of the top-rated tourist locations in Israel, so even if it isn't the perfect time of the year to celebrate, there's so much to see, experience, and enjoy in Haifa.

In Haifa, Israel, a Christmas tree, menorah, and crescent can be found in the city's square during the winter holidays.

ALL THE ARTS

The Jerash Festival for Culture and Arts in Jordan attracts more than 150,000 visitors for evening events. Established by Queen Nour, the aim of the festival is to offer culturally enriching activities, and it has become one of the largest arts and culture events in the Middle East. This cultural carnival was established in 1981 against the backdrop of the Lebanon War. It's an annual summer festival, located in Jerash, then moving to Amman, Karak, Zarqa, Salt, and Irbid—with one of the venues situated in a centuries-old palace in Beiteddine, Lebanon. The Jerash Festival showcases Jordanian and international artists, with music, book exhibits, Shakespearean drama, poetry readings, and dance all staged at venues through-out the cities in temples, public plazas, and, most dramatically, in the fully lighted ancient Byzantine ruins.

Men dress as ancient Roman soldiers during the Jerash Festival.

The coastal resort of El Gouna is the site of Egypt's Sandbox Festival, one of the top must-attend music festivals in the world.

IN THE SANDBOX

Egypt's Sandbox Festival is an annual musical festival established in 2013 at the coastal resort of El Gouna. It's an electronic music extravaganza that brings 40 DJ and live-music performances to this Egyptian paradise for a festival ranging over three days on the Red Sea. The Heineken-sponsored festival is also listed as one of the must-attend festivals, and it is a top selection for bucket lists. The musical talent also interacts with the audiences to contribute to an ever-more-immersive environment. Beach-bound activities include diving, horseback riding, kiting, snorkeling, and windsurfing. With music, sun, party, and surf, what more could anyone ask for?

TASTES OF THE MIDDLE EAST

The Qatar International Food Festival is a springtime celebration of fine foods, cooking classes, theater, and fireworks. The event focuses on the diversity of foods, but it also features a mini zoo, a

The Qatar International Food Festival features more than just food. The event includes a mini zoo, a farmer's market, cultural shows, and more.

farmer's market, cultural shows, fireworks, fitness classes, musical performances, and even a kids' zone. Representative culinary experiences include foods from Ethiopia, the Philippines, South Africa, Lebanon, Ethiopia, Mexico, Turkey, Vietnam, and the United States. Beyond the celebrity chefs and mouth-watering tastings, the Qatar International Food Festival features cooking demos with amazing tips and tricks.

Crowds of people roam the aisles of the Cairo International Book Fair.

CAIRO INTERNATIONAL BOOK FAIR

Even though book events take place around the world, the Cairo International Book Fair is one of the best known, both in the region and internationally. With a mix of lectures, readings, and other book-related activities, the event focuses on Arab-language books more than any other book fair. First established in 1969, it's the oldest book fair in the Middle East, with a regular draw of 1–2 million attendees. More recently, protests and political controversies have become a focus of the event.

The Cairo International Book Fair was canceled in 2011 because of the revolt in Egypt associated with the Arab Spring.

CHAPTER 6 NORTH AMERICA

North American festivals offer a variety of settings and stylings so that every personality or preference can be more than satisfied. There are events that inspire and allow one to listen to new music, experience spectacular sights, or gain insight from others. From Coachella and Lollapalooza to Burning Man and the Fourth of July, there is a festival for everyone in this part of the world.

COACHELLA AND LOLLAPALOOZA

The Coachella Valley Music and Arts Festival is a three-day weekend event held at the Empire Polo Club in Indio, California. Cofounded by Paul Tollett and Rick Van Santen, the first event took place just three months after the second Woodstock festival in 1999, and it was relaunched in 2001. The festival has quickly become one of the most famous and largest international music festivals, with nearly a million attendees. The mix of live music and visual arts (installations and sculpture) have also helped to ensure that the event is one of the most consistently profitable music festivals, but the organizers also focus efforts on minimizing Coachella's carbon footprint by supporting environmental sustainability with a goal of diverting 90 percent of compostable and recyclable materials from landfills.

Lollapalooza is an annual music festival featuring a variety of music stylings, including alternative rock, hip-hop, electronic music, heavy metal, and beyond. The history of the event has been a bit spotty, however, with lapses and a 2003

In addition to music, the Coachella Valley Music and Arts Festival is known for its wild and obscure art installations.

Crowds gather to listen to their favorite bands at Lollapalooza.

revival, but it now draws more than 160,000 people. The name of the festival came from a *Three Stooges* film, meaning something extraordinary, but it also refers to a large lollipop. To many, it's appropriately named on many different levels. The festival has attempted to push the limits of what a music festival is supposed to be—with a focus on touring, it's in a different location every year, not only in the United States but also in international venues. The festival has been criticized for being too corporate.

South by Southwest (SXSW) is an annual festival in Austin, Texas. The event was founded in 1987 by Louis Black, Nick Barbaro, Roland Swenson, and Louis Jay Meyers. The SXSW extravaganza has continued to evolve, with additions in different areas of music, film, and interactive media, and it continues to grow by leaps and bounds. The overall numbers of attendees for the series of festivals over the 10 days now reaches more than 200,000. The festival is not containable and has grown into comedy and gaming topic areas, with its finger on the pulse of popular and programmatically successful content. With the continued growth, critics have lambasted SXSW for many of the side effects of fast and uncontrolled growth. Problems with the huge crowds, violence, and safety concerns are ever-present, as they are with other huge festivals. With the free-and-easy artistic vibe that imbues the festival (at least in branding), critics also lament the level of commercialization.

FINDING HALLOWEEN

Halloween, also known as All Hallows' Eve, Allhallowtide, or All Saints' Eve, is celebrated throughout North America. It's a time for trick-or-treating, dressing up in costumes, and lighting bonfires. On a more scary, thrill-seeking level, it's about ghosts, goblins, and haunted houses, with horror stories and films being ever-popular attractions. Samhain, a Celtic festival, is often closely tied to modern conceptions of Halloween, with its relation to harvest and the encroaching winter. Because the days were shorter, spirits could more easily travel between the realms, which also contributed to the spooky, even scary, connection with the darkest days of the year. The people used candles, prayer, and rituals to ward off evil—bringing light to the darkness. The influence of Christianity on the festival is also evident.

In the fifteenth century, children went door-to-door collecting soul cakes at Allhallowtide. The people would dress up as saints, and then they'd carve and display jack-o-lanterns to represent the souls of the dead. With all the ties to religious and pagan practices and beliefs, the Halloween festivities naturally accompanied the colonists to the New World. The Puritans were anti-Halloween, just as they were against the Christmas tradition, but other immigrants continued their

On All Hallows' Eve, children take to the streets yelling "Trick or treat!" in hopes of getting candy.

At Halloween parties, children will dress up and often play games like Bobbing for Apples.

familiar traditions, intermingling and changing them with Native American harvest festivals as well as celebrations from other international influences into a melting pot of shared cultural experience. In particular, Scottish and Irish immigrants helped to shape the Halloween celebrations in North America with bobbing apples, fortune-telling, reading ghost stories, and setting off fireworks. The practice of dressing in disguise or costume and going trick-or-treating may have also evolved as a mischievous American iteration of the English Guy Fawkes Day.

The "trick" aspect of Halloween was controversial, because it could involve criminal activity, property damage, and even assault, but community and social organizations also organized Halloween festivals and carnivals to mitigate bad behavior. Anoka, Minnesota, has claimed the title "Halloween Capital of the World"—it was the first recorded city to host a Halloween celebration with costumes, a parade, tons of treats (popcorn, peanuts, and candy), and a bonfire. Of course, Salem, Massachusetts, contests Anoka's claim (and title). The annual Halloween celebrations have continued since 1920 (with the exception of 1942–1943 during World War II). Halloween festivities are now celebrated in most communities across the United States as well as other countries around the world.

CELEBRATING DIVERSITY

Burning Man is an annual festival in Black Rock City, a temporary city in Nevada that springs up for the event. It's hot, dry, and dusty in the tent city, but that hasn't stopped nearly 100,000 attendees from converging on the location every year since 1986. They show up in the desert to participate in artistic expression and experimentation in its many forms, including music, elaborate sculptures, and mutant cars. Clothing is optional, it seems. The ever-present central symbol of the festival is the "burning man." The founder, Larry Harvey, said that the burning man never had any influence from "wicker man" customs and rituals, which involve burning live sacrifices. Initially, it was just a bunch of sticks tied together, but the building materials and process has become more elaborate.

As is common with free-thinking and free-expression get-togethers, Burning Man promotes environmentally safe practices, including "leave no trace," which encourages each person to consciously choose practices that have the least possible impact on the environment and are sustainable. In more general situations, "leave no trace" involves disposing of waste in an appropriate, noninvasive way (for example, packing out any garbage or unnatural human refuse), and also leaving the area the same way you found it (without building structures or removing rocks). Other philosophical underpinnings for the event include decommodification based on gifting (no money exchanges hands), inclusion, and self-reliance. Unfortunately, even with the focus on environmental responsibility, the festival has an enormous

The Burning Man Festival is notorious for its artistic expression. In 2016, the festival featured an art installation of an old Boeing 747.

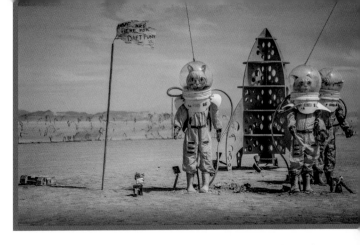

carbon footprint (thousands of vehicles all enter the same small area). From an environmentally conscious point of view, "leave no trace" sounds great but the reality of the festival falls very short of its ideal sustainable, zero-waste goals. Sustainability is encouraged and applauded in the Burning Man campsites, but ultimately attendees leave behind hundreds of thousands of plastic water bottles when they pack up and go home. Municipalities in the United States (like Concord, Massachusetts), in Canada, and in Australia have banned the use of plastic water bottles, and concerned and environmentally individuals consciously use sustainable bottles. The organizers of Burning Man would likely be forced to completely ban plastic water bottles to ensure that they were encouraging the most sustainable and environmentally conscious event possible, but without such a policy, they continue to be criticized by nonprofit organizations like the Sierra Club for their devastating mess.

Burning Man revelers dress in a variety of outfits for the festival.

Why Are Fireworks So Important on July 4th?

The general consensus is that fireworks were first invented in China, with a mixture of sulfur, saltpeter, and charcoal, although some historians point to India or even the Middle East. For the Chinese, the discovery of rudimentary gunpowder was achieved in their search for eternal life (their very own explosive fountain of youth), but it appeared to work well to scare evil spirits away when bamboo shoots stuffed with gunpowder were thrown into the fire, or paper cylinders were lighted with fuses.

The Chinese turned fireworks into bombs and rockets, and then Marco Polo brought fireworks back to Europe in 1295, which took royal entertainment displays to the next level. Pyrotechnics evolved through the Renaissance, as the Italians used chemicals to create new display colors. The first fireworks display in the New World was probably set off by Captain John Smith, but dramatic fireworks became a Fourth of July tradition when they were set off on the one-year anniversary of the adoption of the Declaration of Independence, on July 4, 1777.

AMERICA'S FOURTH OF JULY

It's known as Independence Day in America, and the Fourth of July offers a series of spectacular celebrations across the 50 states. The purpose of the day is to commemorate the nation's birthday, and the true beginning was in 1776 when the Continental Congress voted for independence on July 2 and then adopted the Declaration of Independence on July 4. With those few days of wiggle room, debate has surfaced about the correct day to celebrate U.S. Independence. John Adams was one of the most famous proponents for national celebration on July 2 instead. Now Independence Day is imbued with a rich and varied history of fireworks, apple pie, and festivities of every possible variety.

Every year, Macy's puts on a display of fireworks in New York City for the Fourth of July.

STILL GIVING THANKS

Thanksgiving Day is an annual event celebrated in the United States, Canada, Liberia, Grenada, and Saint Lucia. Canadian Thanksgiving may have originated in 1578 with the voyage of the English explorer Martin Frobisher, or it may have begun as a harvest festival by French settlers in the seventeenth century. The event evolved from the early days of sharing food with the indigenous people of Canada, and it picked up rituals and traditions as German, Irish, and Scottish immigrants joined the celebration.

Pilgrim and Puritan immigrants launched the U.S.-based Thanksgiving holiday in 1619, based on a London Company dictate that they celebrate an annual day of thanksgiving. A feast at the Plymouth colony in 1621 followed, inspired by a bountiful harvest, but it later set off a historical debate about the true origins of the first American Thanksgiving. Though there were harvest festivals throughout New England during this period, President George Washington finally proclaimed November 26, 1789, as the first national day of Thanksgiving. As further fuel for the flames of controversy, some historians point to earlier Thanksgiving celebrations by Spanish explorers in 1565 or 1598.

In North America, Thanksgiving is often spent with family, or those closest to us, with large amounts of food—especially turkey!

TAKING TO THE SKIES AND SEAS

The Albuquerque Balloon Fiesta is an international event that attracts nearly a million people to watch the ascension of more than 600 hot air balloons in Albuquerque's box canyon, which features predictable wind patterns at different elevations. The combination of ideal cold temperature and unique winds combine to allow balloonists to ascend, move in a southerly direction, and then descend to lower elevations to move northward.

The Balloon Fiesta is a nine-day celebration that was first launched in 1972, with dawn ascensions and evening balloon-glow events. The colorful extravaganza also offers balloon races, food booths, and other local balloon-related events and activities at the Anderson-Abruzzo Albuquerque International Balloon Museum and Balloon Fiesta Park. When the weather is good (not pouring rain or too windy), the sky fills up with ascending balloons of every color, special shape, and personality—from Darth Vader, the Creamland milk cow, a giant spider, Garfield, Humpty Dumpty, the Wells Fargo wagon, Yoda, Elvis, Red the Angry Bird, Vincent van Gogh, and SpongeBob.

The Albuquerque Balloon Festival is a sight to see. Hundreds of hot air balloons in various shapes and sizes take flight.

REMEMBERING VETERANS ON MEMORIAL DAY

Veterans Day (formerly Armistice Day) is a national holiday on November 11th each year. It was originally established to recognize the end of World War I. Legislation later expanded the recognition to honor American veterans from all wars. Australia, Canada, France, and Great

Veterans Day is a time to thank and remember those who have served to protect our freedoms. Often, parades are held to honor them.

Britain all commemorate World War I and II veterans. In the United States, Veterans Day brings parades, veteran-appreciation events, and parties.

Federal offices are closed on Veterans Day, as are other offices, schools, and different businesses, but much the same can be said for Memorial Day, which is also a U.S.-based national holiday. Indeed, Memorial Day is often confused with Veterans Day. To be clear, Memorial Day is set aside to remember those who have lost their lives in service to the country as part of the U.S. military, whereas Veterans Day honors all those who served in the armed forces.

The Gathering of Nations is one of the largest Native American powwows in North America.

THE GATHERING OF NATIONS

The Gathering of Nations draws more than 3,000 participants to Albuquerque, New Mexico, for two days of singing, dancing, and other performances, distinguishing the event as the largest powwow in North America. The Gathering first convened in 1983, and it has continued to grow. It now represents more than 700 Native American tribes from the United States and Canada. The trader's market and street fair contribute to the immersive experience, with more than 800 artists and crafters participating. Traditional ritual and dance make way for a parade of horses, recognizing the role of the horse in many tribal cultures. Contemporary culture melds with ritual and tradition as the Gathering of the Nations continues to support an annual literacy program. The Gathering also sponsors a traveling show, a community outreach effort that includes performances held around the world.

ALOHA FESTIVALS

Hula dancers perform at the annual Aloha Festival.

The Aloha Festivals draw more than a million people to a month-long series of events in Hawaii. Former members of the Junior Chamber of Commerce first established the event as Aloha Week in 1946, to encourage a celebration of Hawaii's rich and diverse heritage with street parties, music concerts, dances, historical presentations, and parades. It's designed to be free and easily accessible by the public, with activities that encourage participants to learn more about Hawaiian culture and history, centering around the Aloha Festival Royal Court, which presides over events. In keeping with tradition, festival highlights also include the hula *kahiko* (ancient hula) and chanting.

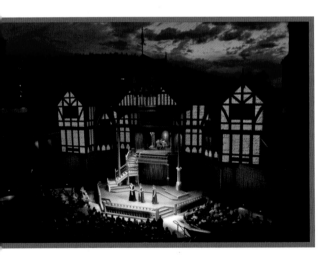

Performers take the stage at the outdoor Elizabethan Theater at the Shakespeare Festival.

MUCH ADO ABOUT THE FESTIVAL

The Oregon Shakespeare Festival (OSF) convenes in Ashland, Oregon, for an eight-month season of award-winning performances of both classic and modern plays—including those of William Shakespeare, of course. The festival has produced 11 plays each year since it presented its first theatrical performances in 1935, but it has also become the center of a unique cultural experience.

Like other festivals and theatrical events, participants can tap into backstage tours as well as access lectures, classes, workshops, and more. The buildings have been designed and built up to accommodate the special theatrical requirements of classic playwrights (the OSF has the oldest full-scale Elizabethan stage in the Western Hemisphere), as well as the more flexible and immersive demands of contemporary artists.

CHAPTER 7 OCEANIA

Festivals in Oceania offer some of the most eclectic, but at the same time utterly spectacular, views and experiences, ranging from historical reenactments and Mad Hatter tea parties to Aboriginal dance festivals, while never straying far from more modern experiences, such as high-flying balloon adventures and seaside food fests.

ABORIGINAL AUSTRALIA

The Garma Festival of Traditional Cultures takes place on Arnhem Land, in Australia. "Garma" is the indigenous equivalent of the World Economic Forum, with the goal of engaging leaders, intellectuals, and journalists to discuss Australian issues. The festival celebrates the Yolngu aboriginal people, drawing attendees from more than 20 cultural groups to create to a completely immersive cultural experience. The event was first convened in 1998 to preserve, educate, and share Yolngu aboriginal culture, which is more than 50,000 years old. The event regularly draws 2,500 people for music, art, and storytelling, along with a film program and exhibits. Designed to be fun and entertaining, the focus is also on providing youth with a wide range of important tools that give them a voice, including education in journalism, social media, and writing.

But the Garma Festival is not the only aboriginal festival in the region. The Laura Dance Festival is one of the biggest gatherings of aboriginal and Torres

The Yolngu people dance during the Garma Festival.

Strait Islander people in Australia. This biannual event celebrates 40,000 years of culture, with over 500 artists, and it draws more than 5,000 attendees to each three-day festival event. Like Garma, the Laura Dance Festival features workshops, displays, and art exhibitions, along with games and entertainment for kids.

The Yabun Festival joins the Garma and the Laura Dance Festival as an important aboriginal festival, but it convenes for just one day each year, in Sydney. This event was launched in 2001, and even though it's only a day-long event, it still features forums on aboriginal issues and the ever-popular performances by indigenous dance groups. The event also features a marketplace of indigenous items, including clothes, jewelry, arts and crafts, and food. A focus is also on the kids: Jarjum's Tent features storytelling, arts and crafts, and book readings by indigenous authors.

The Laura Dance Festival is another aboriginal festival held in Australia.

The Tjungu Festival is a four-day event that takes place in April in celebration of Australian aboriginal culture. This festival converges on Ayers Rock Resort for traditional bush food, art, and indigenous music. It also features the Tjungu Indigenous Short Film Festival, the Tjungu Fashion Parade, and the ever-popular AFL Tjungu Cup, featuring local Australian-rules football teams.

A DAY FOR AUSTRALIA

Australia Day (also called Foundation Day, Anniversary Day, Survival Day, or Invasion Day) is the official national day that honors Australia. It celebrates the day when the so-called First Fleet landed at Port Jackson in 1788, and the British declared sovereignty over Australia's eastern seaboard (known as New Holland). In keeping with the importance of such a historical event, it's a time of picnics, get-togethers, fireworks, and citizenship ceremonies. The first event took place back in 1808, although official recognition for the day didn't happen until 1935.

Although indigenous events like the Woggan-ma-gule Ceremony are now included as part of the festivities, controversy also surrounds what some aboriginal Australians consider to be an invasion. Indeed, the aboriginal peoples

Revelers celebrate Australia Day with displays of their country's flag, in addition to get-togethers, picnics, fireworks, and citizenship ceremonies.

The Australian prime minister hands out citizenship certificates to new Australian citizens on Australia Day.

call it Invasion Day, as they mourn the loss of indigenous culture and advocate for a change in the national holiday. They also call it Survival Day, a time to celebrate the fact that indigenous people survived, despite the odds. Starting in 2017, several city councils (Yarra, Darebin, and Byron Shire) resolved to no longer recognize Australia Day and instead host events that highlight aboriginal history and culture. The federal government punished the cities by refusing to allow them to conduct citizen ceremonies going forward. With the depth of hurtful controversy, but also because of the wide and varied history of the region, calls for debate on date-change options have arisen. But politicians have been unwilling to broach the subject. Prime Minister John Howard did acknowledge the concerns in 2001, but even he was unwilling to circumvent what he called such a significant day in Australian history.

AUSTRALIA'S SPRING SPECTACULARS

The Toowoomba Carnival of Flowers features beautiful displays like this one.

The Oceania region features a whole series of well-established festivals that celebrate spring, with wild profusions of flowers, music, and art. The Toowoomba Carnival of Flowers is a 10-day international festival in Queensland, held every September since 1949. Sure, this celebration of spring includes live music from Australia's top performers, but there's also wine, workshops, food, and show rides. It all kicks off with the Heritage Bank Festival of Food and Wine, but it doesn't end there. The Carnival really is a thing. Rides, games, and carnival food (fairy floss, or cotton candy, and dagwood dogs, which are similar to American corndogs) are available down Sideshow Alley in Lower Queens Park.

The Grand Central Floral Parade leads the show to Queens Park, with more than 70 floral floats, street performers, live bands, carousel rides, and colorful characters. It's fun for adults as well as kids, as they collect chalk and take to the streets to show off their creativity or stop off at the petting zoo or sandpit. Against the floral backdrop, there's also arts and crafts activities designed to encourage personal exploration and invention through take-away projects and fun design challenges. The event was originally

created to boost the tourism trade after the World War II, but it has evolved into a blockbuster event that is growing in popularity, with more than 250,000 attendees at last count.

The Kings Park Festival is a celebration of the wildflowers of Western Australia—just in time for spring. Since 1964, the month-long

Families enjoy the rows of tulips during the Tesselaar Tulip Festival.

event has attracted 500,000 visitors, who enjoy the art, photography, workshops, live music, lawn games, exhibits, walking tours, and, of course, flowers. Beyond the sights, sounds, and flavors of spring, this event offers something a bit different. It's an opportunity to slow down, relax, and meditate—the wellness activities include classes in meditation, tai chi, and yoga.

Although it would appear to be the antithesis of the Kings Park Festival, the Tesselaar Tulip Festival features a series of events in celebration of spring, but varied in their themes, with the Tulips in Wonderland Week, a Turkish Weekend, a Dutch Weekend, and an Irish Weekend just a few of the focal areas. With such a wide range of event possibilities, with the added benefit of seeing the blooming tulips at the same time, the *Alice in Wonderland*–themed party offers just the right amount of mad-hattery to suit most curiosities. The Wonderland event even features photo ops with the book's characters, storytelling, live music, and even a Mad Hatter's High Tea. Who doesn't love a good Lewis Carroll tie-in?

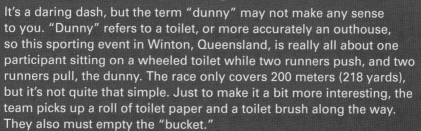

Australian Dunny Derby

It's a daring dash, but the term "dunny" may not make any sense to you. "Dunny" refers to a toilet, or more accurately an outhouse, so this sporting event in Winton, Queensland, is really all about one participant sitting on a wheeled toilet while two runners push, and two runners pull, the dunny. The race only covers 200 meters (218 yards), but it's not quite that simple. Just to make it a bit more interesting, the team picks up a roll of toilet paper and a toilet brush along the way. They also must empty the "bucket."

BEYOND THE FRINGE FEST

The Adelaide Festival blends music, dance, arts, and drama into an extravaganza of sights and sounds, which includes the Fringe Fest and WOMADelaide, as part of the Mad March. If you've ever heard the saying "mad as a March hare," that's what Mad March is all about. It's the time of year when unexpected, crazy, or unusual antics might happen, specifically in allusion to the breeding season but much broader in general usage. As an event in Australia, it was first launched in 1960. Now, the event features more than 1,000 events across Adelaide's parks and warehouses, as well as more well-established venues. The month-long festival includes magic, comedy, drama, music, and art displays. WOMADelaide is a 1992 spin-off of the original World of Music, Arts, and Dance (WOMAD) festival, which was first launched in 1980 in Shepton Mallet, UK. Since then WOMAD events have been held at numerous locations around the world, entertaining more than a million people.

On the other side of the Australian continent, the Vivid Sydney festival runs for 23 days, with displays of lights and music. The spectacular art sculptures, light displays, and projections make this one of the world's largest outdoor galleries. The event was launched in 2009 as a lighting festival. Mary-Anne Kyriakou was originally inspired by a German lighting fair. It now draws more than 2 million attendees every year. The interactive and immersive aspects of the displays and exhibits contribute to the continued fame and financial success of Vivid Sydney.

Crowds gather to listen to the symphony and watch fireworks at the Adelaide Festival.

TAKE TO THE BEACH, CANOE, AND SURF

Oceania is a series of islands, so it's not a surprise that some of the most memorable events in the region relate to the beach and surf. The Rip Curl Pro Bells Beach (formerly Bells Beach Surf Classic) is an annual surfing event. Based in Bells Beach, Victoria, Australia, it's a world-tour surfing competition. The event was established in 1961, and it went pro in 1973.

Yap is a small island state in Micronesia. The Canoe Festival was established in 2009 as a celebration of Yapese sailing culture, with racing, dancing, food, a parade of traditional sailing canoes, and other competitions. It takes place at the Yap Living History Museum grounds, featuring demonstrations in bamboo raft making as well as weaving (sails and coconut husk rope).

The Fish and Sips Seafood Festival (formerly the Fremantle Seafood Festival) is just about what the name suggests: seafood. With an ever-growing fan base of avid seafood lovers, the event draws more than 20,000 people to Fremantle, Western Australia, for award-winning wine and seafood platters. What's even more fun is the combination of music and cooking demos, including master classes.

Surfers take part in the Rip Curl Pro Bells Beach contest.

CAMELS IN THE OUTBACK

Camel events are famous in Africa, the Middle East, and in many other parts of the world, but they're also part of festivals in Australia. The Uluru Camel Cup is an event that was established in 2012 as part of a series of community events, including Outback Week and the Outback Fest. While the financial

Camel racing may seem odd, but it is a common event held in Australia.

significance is important, the festival also taps into Australia's history and culture to reinforce the lasting importance of the camel, though the animals were brought to the continent only in the mid-nineteenth century.

Camel racing is often misinterpreted and underappreciated, which means that beyond a time of fun, parties, and laughter, the racing event is designed to change the public's perception of such events. Although camels are not as essential to subsistence in the hot and dry climate as they were in the past, they've still proven that they have a part to play in Australian society.

COMMEMORATION AND MEMORIAL IN AUSTRALIA AND NEW ZEALAND

The Australian War Memorial lists the names of those lost. In remembrance of the dead, visitors leave red poppies on Anzac Day.

Anzac Day (ANZAC stands for Australian and New Zealand Army Corps) is one of the most important national events in Australia—it marks the first major campaign fought in 1914 by Australian and New Zealand military forces during World War I—the infamous Gallipoli Campaign. The campaign was a failure, with the loss of more than 8,709 Australian soldiers, 2,779 New Zealand soldiers, and 21,255 soldiers from the United Kingdom (Great Britain and Ireland). The day is an important memorial to the bravery and sacrifice of the men who fought. The commemoration has been expanded to include all Australians and New Zealanders who served and died in times of war. As a national observance, the event includes services at dawn as well as commemorative marches and remembrance services. The Australia Post has also issued a series of postal stamps in recognition of Anzac Day and the specific wars that have been fought.

BEYOND DIRT AND HEIVA

Polynesian dancers during the Heiva in Bora Bora.

The Julia Creek Dirt n Dust Festival is a three-day sporting event that is in a class by itself as one of the biggest festivals in Queensland. The event takes place in April, with a series of competitions, races, and live events. More than 3,000 people are drawn to the dust festival, perhaps at least in part because of the tough-as-nails triathlon, as well as the bull rides, horse races, and snorkeling. Perhaps most off-kilter of all is the Best Butt Competition—for men and women.

The Heiva is a month-long festival in Tahiti that celebrates Polynesian culture. In Tahitian, *heiva* means "to assemble" and "community places," so the event brings together artists, dancers, and singers in an island paradise. The origins of the festival is particularly remarkable, since King Pomare II banned all dancing in 1819. Although dancing was finally allowed for official functions (military parades and torch-lit processions) in 1881, it wasn't until 1961 that troupes were really allowed to perform.

The farmers already had the pumpkins, so a pumpkin festival was organized to support the local economy and provide some fun.

ROLLING PUMPKINS

The Goomeri Pumpkin Festival was first held in 1997 in Queensland, Australia, because the drought that year was depressing and economically devastating to the country. What better way to cheer everyone up and support the local economy than to host a fun festival, particularly since farmers already had the pumpkins? The pumpkin-rolling content sounds a bit like England's Cooper's Hill Cheese-Rolling and Wake, but to the townspeople it sounded off-kilter and impossible. Participants rolled 72 pumpkins down the Policeman's Hill in the first festival. The first event drew 1,000 attendees, but the success also encouraged the town to continue and even expand the festival with events like the quilt challenge, pageant, tea towel competition, shot put, and decorated pumpkins, along with a parade, entertainment, and pumpkin food.

AMONG US

The Cardwell UFO Festival was first convened in 2014 to discuss sightings like Tully Saucer Nests and the Cardwell Lights. It's the only unidentified flying object event in Australia, and it has been listed as one of the top 10 festivals for UFO lovers. It's an unusual event, but it regularly draws people from around the world. With

The beautiful seaside town of Cardwell in North Queensland, Australia, hosts an annual UFO festival.

open discussions, live entertainment, a car rally, scavenger hunt, an auction, and a lantern parade, the Cardwell UFO Festival offers activities for every possible interest level and most age categories. The whole event is set against a backdrop of beautiful beaches.

The Canberra Balloon Spectacular truly is spectacular. Balloons shaped like birds, frogs, and others fly high above the ground.

TAKE TO THE SKIES

The Canberra Balloon Spectacular is an international balloon festival that features more than 50 hot-air balloons taking to the air from the lawn of old Parliament House over a series of nine days in the autumn (March). Like the Albuquerque Balloon Festival in the United States, the Canberra Festival features a "special shapes" event, as well as live music, activities, entertainment, and food. The event regularly draws more than 30,000 attendees and is one of the top four balloon festivals in the world. That's partially due to the gorgeous scenery of Lake Burley Griffin and Mount Ainslie.

Attendees camp at the lake, rent a boat to get an even more spectacular experience, or just stand by to take in the views during the early-morning ascents. A few side trips are then in order, because as Australia's capital city, Canberra offers a range of spectacular art and entertainment venues that perfectly complement and enhance the ballooning experience. The National Gallery of Australia features 7,500 Aboriginal, Asian, and Australian artwork across 13 galleries. The Floriade NightFest also offers a unique look at the city parkland in Australia's biggest celebration of spring (September–October).

FURTHER READING & INTERNET RESOURCES

BOOKS

Bunson, Margaret. *Encyclopedia of Ancient Egypt.* 3rd ed. New York: Facts on File, 2012. Based on her research and interest in ancient Egypt, Margaret Bunson compiles 2,300 entries that include many of the latest discoveries in addition to well-established scholarship.

Cohen, Ronald. *A History of Folk Music Festivals in the United States.* Lanham, MD: Scarecrow Press, 2008. Ronald Cohen covers music events and festivals in North America, offering insights and descriptions that encompass a wide range of musical styles.

Davidson, Alan. *The Oxford Companion to Food.* Oxford: Oxford University Press, 1999. The most prominent international food festivals offer an exploration of history, culture, and unique expertise—and that's what this book offers. It's a celebration of food from around the world.

Galvan, Javier. *They Do What?: A Cultural Encyclopedia of Extraordinary and Exotic Customs from around the World.* Santa Barbara, CA: ABC-CLIO, 2014. Javier Galvan highlights unusual customs involving birth, death, and everything in between. Entries by 48 authors explore festivals, food, religion, and more.

Salamone, Frank. *Routledge Encyclopedia of Religious Rites, Rituals, and Festivals.* New York, NY: Routledge, 2004. From Easter and Divali to Ramadan and Yom Kipper, this encyclopedia offers 130 entries on religious and secular rituals from around the world.

WEB SITES

www.greenglobaltravel.com/top-10-festivals-in-the-world/. Green Global Travel describes the top 10 festivals in the world that you may want to visit one day.

www.bugbog.com/. *BugBog* is defined as a "bruise" from Proto-Malayo-Polynesian origin. The site offers reviews and details about internationally renowned festivals, categorized by Music, European, UK, American, Exotic, and Arts events. BugBog also includes tips about health and safety, as well as information on how to get there on the cheap.

www.buzzfeed.com/ashleyperez/23-world-festivals-you-wont-want-to-miss. In this *Buzzfeed* article, "23 World Festivals You Won't Want To Miss," Ashley Perez offers quick lists of festivals from around the world, with photos that offer additional inspiration to fly right into those international adventures.

www.pitchfork.com/festivals/. *Pitchfork* is an online magazine that features news and features, and the "Pitchfork Guide to Festivals" provides links and details for music festivals from around the world. The site was first launched in 1995 by Ryan Schreiber, and it is owned by the media company Condé Nast.

INDEX

AUTHOR'S BIOGRAPHY

Esther Lombardi is a full-time author and journalist. She earned a master's degree in English literature from California State University, Sacramento, with postgraduate coursework in web technology from the University of Oregon. She draws from her background to create fun and compelling articles and stories.

CREDITS

COVER

(clockwise from top left) Burning Man, Black Rock Desert, USA, Lukas Bischoff/Dreamstime; Carnival, Venice, Italy, Colombo Nicola/Shutterstock; Junkanoo, Nassau, the Bahamas, Erkki $ Hanna/Shutterstock; Guerewol Festival, Agadez, Niger, Homo Cosmicos/Shutterstock; Lollapalooza, Santiago, Chile, ampueroleonardo/iStock; Holi, Jaipur, India, Luca Roggero/Dreamstime

INTERIOR

1, Radu Razvan/Shutterstock; 2–3, Natallia Charkesava/Dreamstime; 5, Dmitry Rukhlenko/Shutterstock; 9, isaxar/Shutterstock; 10, Homo Cosmicos/Shutterstock; 11, Homo Cosmicos/Shutterstock; 12, Aissa Xinhua News Agency/Newscom; 13, erichon/Shutterstock; 14, Alvaro Villanueva/Shutterstock; 15, WitR/Shutterstock; 16, Chine Nouvelle/Sipa/Newscom; 17, Homo Cosmicos/Shutterstock; 18, Pan Chaoyue/Newscom; 19 (UP), Hari Karki/Shutterstock; 19 (LO), Marina Campbell/Dreamstime; 20 (UP), Nomwindé/Wikimedia Commons; 20 (LO), Serge Dibert/Newscom; 21, Anastasia Mazeina/Shutterstock; 22, Chanont Kemthong/Shutterstock; 23, winhorse/iStock; 24, Dipak Shelare/Shutterstock; 25, Mikadun/Shutterstock; 26, Vladimir Goncharenko/Shutterstock; 27, Artography/Shutterstock; 28, Eugene Ga/Shutterstock; 29, Mariusz Jurgielewicz/Dreamstime; 30, MartineDF/Shutterstock; 31 (UP), Sean Pavone/Shutterstock; 31 (LO), Ba Tung Huynh/Shutterstock; 32 (UP), yochika photographer/Shutterstock; 32 (LO), Zaini Ahmat/Dreamstime; 33, EngravingFactory/Shutterstock; 34, imagestockdesign/Shutterstock; 35, Aandbphotos/Dreamstime; 36, Dmitry Chulov/Dreamstime; 37, Ms Deborah Waters/Shutterstock; 38, Roberto Zilli/Shutterstock; 39, MeAroundtheworld/Shutterstock; 40, Melodia plus photos/Shutterstock; 41, Iakov Filimonov/Shutterstock; 42, Sergio Delle Vedove/Dreamstime; 43 (UP), Vladimir Zhoga/Shutterstock; 43 (LO), noel bennett/Shutterstock; 44 (UP), anandoart/Shutterstock; 44 (LO), David Ortega Baglietto/Shutterstock; 45, Jiewsurreal/Shutterstock; 46, CP DC Press/Shutterstock; 47, sunsinger/Shutterstock; 48, Don Mammoser/Shutterstock; 49, Milton Rodriguez/Shutterstock; 50, jo Crebbin/Shutterstock; 51, Svetlana Day/Dreamstime; 52, poolps27/Shutterstock; 53, Anton_Ivanov/Shutterstock; 54, Barna Tanko/Dreamstime; 55, Gábor Basch/Dreamstime; 56 (UP), Steve Painter/Dreamstime; 56 (LO), Chensiyuan/Wikimedia Commons; 57, A-Gallery/Shutterstock; 58, Edward Karaa/Dreamstime; 59, Le-Dantu Michel/Shutterstock; 60, Manish Jaisi/Shutterstock; 61, Kertu/Shutterstock; 62, Syariff Hidayatullah/Shutterstock; 63, reddees/Shutterstock; 64, point of light/Shutterstock; 65, Irina Opachevsky/Dreamstime; 66, meunierd/Shutterstock; 67, Arsty/Dreamstime; 68 (UP), Imran's Photography/Shutterstock; 68 (LO), Mohd Tarmizi/Wikimedia Commons; 69, SS1001/Shutterstock; 70, sachoben/Wikimedia Commons; 71, Aneil Lutchman/Wikimedia Commons; 72, Monkey Business Images/Shutterstock; 73, Sean Locke Photography/Shutterstock; 74, Jelle Krings/Dreamstime; 75, Jelle Krings/Dreamstime; 76, Winston Tan/Shutterstock; 77, fstop123/iStock; 78, Kobby Dagan/Shutterstock; 79 (UP), Anthony Correia/Shutterstock; 79 (LO), aceshot1/Shutterstock; 80 (UP), Ivansabo/Dreamstime; 80 (LO), Amy Richard/Wikimedia Commons; 81, Rose Makin/Shutterstock; 82, J Mundy/Shutterstock; 83, Anni Mac/Shutterstock; 84, katacarix/Shutterstock; 85, DIAC images/Wikimedia Commons; 86, Ian Scott/Shutterstock; 87, Norman Allchin/Shutterstock; 88, amophoto_au/Shutterstock; 89, Susinder/Dreamstime; 90 (UP), Kritsana_H/Shutterstock; 90 (LO), katacarix/Shutterstock; 91 (UP), Stephan Debelle Duplan/Dreamstime; 91 (LO), Eugene Sim Junying/Dreamstime; 92 (UP), Grant Phillips/Dreamstime; 92 (LO), katacarix/Shutterstock